CONFLICT AND [illegible] AT DURHAM

Four Talks delivered to
the Friends of Durham Cathedral,
2001-02

David Marcombe
Brian Crosby
Christopher Downs
Anne Orde

ISBN 0-9544825-0-6

Published by Friends of Durham Cathedral and printed in Great Britain by Prontaprint, Durham

Cover photograph by kind permission of Mr J. D. Whittaker

Preface

In the winter season of 2001-2002 the Friends of Durham Cathedral heard a series of talks on the theme of 'Conflict and Disaster at Durham'. The text of those talks is now published here: Dr David Marcombe on the much-reviled Dean Whittingham, his acts, his quarrels and the accusations brought against him; Dr Brian Crosby on the controversy about the form of worship, and particularly the use of music, between John Cosin and Peter Smart, brought to a head by the latter's verbal assault from the pulpit; Mr Christopher Downs, the Cathedral Architect, on the conservation policies adopted by his predecessors at the end of the eighteenth century; and Dr Anne Orde on the Chapter's part in the political controversy and demand for Church reform in the early nineteenth century, ending in the foundation of Durham University and the pruning of the cathedral's excessive wealth. It is hoped that Friends who heard the talks will be glad to have copies to refresh their memories, and that others who could not be present will enjoy reading for the first time about these spirited episodes in the history of post-Reformation Durham.

Lilian Groves
Secretary, Friends of Durham Cathedral
April 2003

CONTENTS

'A Great Villain of the Geneva Gang'? William Whittingham, Dean of Durham: a reassessment

David Marcombe

I have always had a great affection for William Whittingham, who was Dean of Durham between 1563 and 1579. I first encountered him during my undergraduate studies at the University of York in the 1960s; followed him through with my Ph.D. here at the University of Durham in the 1970s; and in these last couple of years I have come back to him as his biographer for the new *Dictionary of National Biography*. One of my great regrets is that we have no portrait of him – we have no idea what he looked like – but we do have a signature and there is sufficient documentary evidence to build up a good picture of the sort of man he was; particularly a short biography written soon after his death and published in *The Camden Miscellany* in 1871.

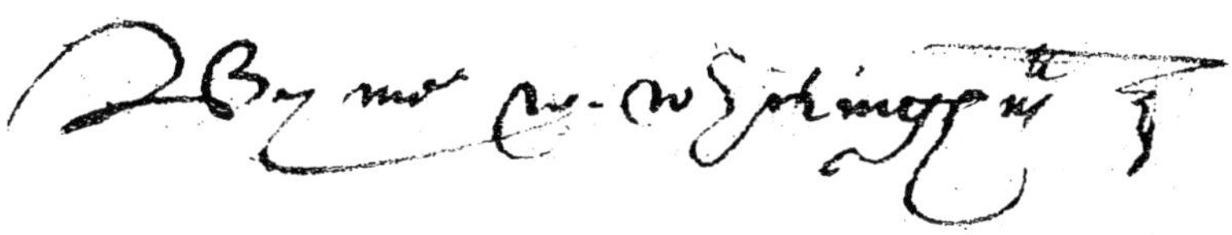

William Whittingham's signature

Though that biography was broadly favourable to Whittingham, the more generalised historical tradition, and in particular the Durham antiquarian tradition, has not treated him so well. To the eighteenth century Tory establishment he was 'a great villain of the Geneva gang' and 'a rank Whig';[1] and William Hutchinson, in his influential *History of Durham,* believed him to be guilty of 'profanation' and 'acts of violence and irreligion':

> Dean Whittingham was guilty of much profanation on the pious monuments and sacred remains in this church. The account given by Wood, of those acts of violence and irreligion, is shortly stated to the reader; but antecedent thereto, we beg leave to observe, that, in all ages, and with all people, where

1 J.T. Fowler (ed.), *The Rites of Durham* (Surtees Society, 107; Durham, 1903), p. 169.

> civilisation and the true spirit of religion prevailed, things applied to pious offices and religious ceremonies were held in such veneration, that defiling them and employing them in mean and contemptuous uses, was forbidden and punished.[2]

In short, he deserved no place in Durham's 'annals of the great and good' – a shameful Dean, best consigned to the dustbin of history.

What I should like to do in this lecture is to explore this 'Black Legend' of Dean Whittingham, to try to work out why he was regarded with such general distaste here in Durham and assess what truth, if any, there was in the accusations. I hope we will be able to build a balanced picture of this remarkable man and see him as more than a puritan bogeyman, sent to terrify tender consciences.

Whittingham was undoubtedly a man of many talents and, on the basis of his ability, one of the most remarkable Deans that Durham has ever had. Principally, he was a scholar with an international reputation, particularly skilled in languages. Whilst he was at Geneva in the 1550s he translated the New Testament; assisted with the Geneva Bible; and contributed to Sternhold and Hopkin's book of English psalms, where the initials 'W.W.' still stand as a memorial to him. His version of the 23rd Psalm gives a flavour of his work:

> The Lord is only my support,
> and he that doth me feed;
> How can I then lack any thing
> whereof I stand in need?
> In pastures green he feedeth me
> where I do safely lie,
> And after leads me to the streams
> which run most pleasantly.[3]

If all of this was designed to bring the message of Protestantism before large numbers of people, he contributed in a more modest fashion here at Durham by taking time out of his busy schedule to teach the boys in the grammar school. His skills as a diplomat were equally well known. In his youth he worked as a translator for Sir John Mason, English ambassador in France, and in 1561 he accompanied Francis Russell, Earl of Bedford, on a mission to France to pass on Queen Elizabeth's condolences on the death of Francis II. In the 1570s he was still being spoken of as a possible ambassador to Scotland and even as a replacement for Lord Burghley as Secretary of

---

[2] W. Hutchinson, *The History and Antiquities of the County Palatine of Durham*, vol. 2 (Durham, 1823), p. 188.

[3] *The Whole Book of Psalms Collected into English Metre by Thomas Sternhold, John Hopkins and others* (Cambridge, 1755), Psalm 23 (WW).

State. As a contemporary put it, 'his ableness in all manner of ways cannot be denied by any that have skill'.[4]

Alongside these scholarly and diplomatic achievements, it is perhaps surprising to learn that Whittingham also had the skills of a soldier. In 1562 he accompanied the English army to Le Havre as chaplain to the commander Ambrose Dudley, Earl of Warwick. He did not take on the passive role of modern-day padre. We are told he often preached in his armour and 'when any alarum came ... he would be on the town wall as soon almost as any man'.[5] This manifestation of the Dean as 'action man' survived into his days at Durham. When the Rebellion of the Northern Earls broke out in 1569 he put his military experience to good use, advising the Bishop on the defence of the county; supervising the reconstruction of Newcastle's fortifications; and gathering intelligence for the Earl of Sussex on the Yorkshire borders. Indeed, he only left Durham at the very last moment, 'secret intelligence being brought unto him if he went not away that night he could not pass southward for the bridges would be taken up the next night'.[6]

So here was a man of wide-ranging and rare talents ... which raises the question, why has his reputation suffered so badly? The problem was, of course, all these events were being played out against the controversial backdrop of the English Reformation and in that context Whittingham represented one extreme of the great divide. He was a puritan, and that meant that his actions would be looked on unfavourably by Catholics and, indeed, sometimes by members of his own side. We know nothing of his conversion. Born and brought up as a Catholic in Chester in the 1520s and 1530s, in his later years he said simply he had been 'called from the blindness of idolatry and superstition', probably while he was a student at Oxford in the 1540s.[7] By the 1550s, during the reign of the Catholic Queen Mary, his beliefs were strong enough to force him into exile on the continent, first at Frankfurt (where he became involved with the controversies amongst the English exiles about the 1552 Prayer Book) and then at Geneva (where he worked closely with John Knox, later a leading light in the Scottish Reformation). He became an elder in the English congregation and its minister between 1558 and 1560,

---

4 D. Marcombe, 'The Dean and Chapter of Durham, 1558-1603' (University of Durham, Ph.D. thesis, 1973), p. 83.

5 'Life of Mr William Whittingham, Dean of Durham, from a MS in Antony Wood's Collection, Bodleian Library', *The Camden Miscellany*, 6 (1871), p. 11.

6 *Ibid.*, pp. 24-5.

7 W. Greenwell (ed.), *Wills and Inventories*, 2 (Surtees Soc., 38; Durham, 1860), p. 15.

though his formal ordination was later called into doubt. It seems that at this stage of his life his sympathies veered towards Presbyterianism, the extreme form of Calvinism favoured by the French Huguenots, one of whom, Katherine Jacqueman, he married at Geneva in 1556.

Though Whittingham never wrote much about his views on church polity, they can, I think, be inferred, partly from the introduction he contributed to Christopher Goodman's book, *How Superior Powers Ought to be Obeyed*, in 1558. Directed against rule by the 'regiment of women' (which Goodman and Whittingham identified with Queen Mary), the whole thing backfired in an embarrassing fashion when the Protestant Elizabeth succeeded to the throne later in the same year. The upshot of this was that the new Queen never fully trusted Whittingham, even when his views had mellowed substantially in later life. Serious suspicions always hung over his head. Did he believe in the Royal Supremacy over the church ... especially when it was exercised by a woman? Was he properly ordained and therefore equipped to follow a career in the church back in England? These doubts would normally have been enough to kill any hope of preferment stone dead, but his patron, Ambrose Dudley, Earl of Warwick, prevailed upon the Queen to give him the Deanery of Durham in 1563. From her point of view Durham was far enough away from London and the universities for this undoubtedly talented man to pose not too much of a problem. After all, there were plenty of Papists to work on in the north and blunt the edge of his religious enthusiasms.

If that was the intention of sending Whittingham to Durham, the plan was not wholly successful because in his own time, and particularly after his death, he was perceived to be a problem. To assess the true extent of this we now need to turn to the 'Black Legend' of Dean Whittingham, expressed by Hutchinson and others, and measure him against it. Basically the charges are threefold. First, that he introduced radical puritan practices into Durham Cathedral in defiance of the Act of Uniformity and the 1559 Settlement. Second, that he was an iconoclast who virtually destroyed the historic fabric of the Cathedral. Third, that he engaged in a programme of mismanagement so profound that the Queen had to conduct a Royal Visitation of the Cathedral in 1578 to try to get rid of him. In other words, she should have stuck with her instincts and not listened to the persuasive words of the Earl of Warwick. So, with Dean Whittingham now firmly in the dock, let us look at each of these three areas to see how much, if any, truth there is in them.

In Ward's *Reformation*, written in the eighteenth century, there is a little rhyme which speaks of Whittingham's puritanism and was widely accepted in Hutchinson's time:

Wood, Williams, Whittingham and Sutton
Valued the Prayer Book not a button:
The liturgy they grudg'd to say
And threw the surplice quite away;
Alter'd confession, chang'd the hymns,
For old Jack Hopkin's pithy rhimes.[8]

That Whittingham was a puritan is beyond doubt. His credentials in that respect were very firmly established at Geneva. However, what is debatable is the extent to which he was prepared to try to impose his beliefs on others. His main brush with the law was during the Vestiarian Controversy of the 1560s when the Queen and the Archbishops were attempting to establish conformity in the use of fairly minimal vestments ... something of which Whittingham, and most puritans, disapproved very strongly. In 1565 the Dean wrote to the Earl of Leicester, a notable supporter of puritan clergy, 'God forbid that we by wearing the Pope's attire as a thing but indifferent should seem thereby to consent to their blasphemies and heresies'.[9] Because of attitudes such as this, Whittingham was called to appear before the High Commission court at York in 1566 accused, specifically, of celebrating communion in the Cathedral in 1563 without cope or surplice and walking around the city in a round cap and black Geneva gown. These charges he freely admitted and he was ordered to wear the correct apparel in the future. Interestingly, Whittingham's response to this order appears to have been never again to celebrate communion in the Cathedral.

All of the shreds of evidence we have in fact point to the Dean's growing conservatism after the confrontation of 1566. Vestments appear to have been the norm in the Cathedral; the Book of Common Prayer was in use; and the Dean subscribed to Archbishop Parker's Articles of 1571 apparently without a struggle. An interesting illustration surviving in a Book of Precedents compiled by the diocesan Chancellor, Robert Swift, a notable ally of Dean Whittingham, suggests the use of conventional vestments by members of the Cathedral hierarchy in 1574. Even more telling is a letter written to Whittingham in the same year by Thomas Wood, one of his old Geneva associates, taking him to task because of his lack of reforming endeavour. In the course of this letter Wood stated that he hoped God:

> will not only give you hearty repentance for your backsliding, but also restore you to your former zeal and boldness to

---

[8] Hutchinson, *History of Durham*, vol. 2, p. 190.

[9] J. Strype, *The Life and Acts of Matthew Parker*, vol. 3 (Oxford, 1821), p. 79.

> acknowledge all that truth which heretofore you have taught to others, which I pray God I may live to see and that speedily.[10]

But Wood was flogging a dead horse because the Dean's religious passion was, by then, a spent force. Not only was he imbued with the growing conservatism which comes with age ... there was also a touch of the Vicar of Bray about him. He did not want to lose the valuable and comfortable Deanery of Durham because of rash misbehaviour, especially now that he had a wife and a large family to support. For these very practical reasons the statements of Colligan and others – that he adopted the English Geneva order at Durham and that the Act of Uniformity was 'of none effect' there – must be treated with extreme caution.[11] On the first count we must find the Dean 'Not Guilty'.

With regard to the second charge – that of iconoclasm – virtually all of our evidence comes from a single source, the *Rites of Durham*, written by Catholic sympathisers in the 1590s who were looking back nostalgically to the 'golden age' of the Prior and Convent before the Reformation. So this is hardly impartial evidence. What is the Dean supposed to have done? He incorporated the east end of the old refectory into the Deanery and made a profit of £20 selling lead from the old roof. He proposed the removal of the bells from the Galilee steeple, but acquiesced in a proposal by the 'Catholic' prebendary, Thomas Sparke (a former monk), to create a new peal in the central tower. He took up some of the old grave slabs from the cemetery and redeployed them in building works 'for he could not abide any ancient monuments, nor nothing that appertained to any godly religiousness or monastical life'.[12] Finally, he removed the old holy water stoups into his kitchen, where they were put to use for salting beef and fish 'having a conveyance in the bottoms of them for letting forth the water'.[13]

None of this is actually very shocking and is exactly what you would expect in an institution undergoing rapid and radical change. The old Priory was being turned into a new secular Cathedral, so obviously there was going to be a high degree of rationalisation and re-use. English Heritage had not yet been invented to restrict freedom of action in this respect. What deserves praise rather than condemnation, perhaps, is the fact the some of these old things were

---

[10] P. Collinson, *Letters of Thomas Wood, Puritan*, Institute of Historical Research, Special Supplement, 5 (1960), pp. 6-9.

[11] J.H. Colligan, *The Honourable William Whittingham of Chester* (Chester, 1934), p. 108.

[12] Fowler (ed.), *Rites of Durham*, p. 60.

[13] *Ibid.*, p. 61.

preserved at all (the gravestones and holy water stoups, for example) rather than their being destroyed entirely. Our own track record in the last two hundred years, when we have had some concept of Heritage awareness, has been infinitely worse than that of Dean Whittingham. Consider, for example, the Gothic Revivalists of the nineteenth century who ruthlessly destroyed our precious Prayer Book churches with their communion tables, box pews, west galleries and benefaction boards. And in our own age, churchyards are being rooted up to convert redundant churches into houses, concert halls, office blocks, shopping malls ... you name it, we do it.

What is perhaps even more remarkable than Whittingham as recycler and proto-conservationist, is what he did *not* touch at all during this supposed frenzied rampage. The Cathedral organs (a favourite target for many puritans) were left unmolested, presumably because of the Dean's love of music. And that did not just include dreary Calvinist psalms. He was said to have obtained some of the best compositions from the Queen's Chapel Royal (which may have been verging on the 'Catholic') for use by the Cathedral choir. The Paschal Candlestick, 'a most mighty vast candlestick' used by the monks at Easter, was discovered hidden in a vault after his death.[14] And many of the old stained glass windows similarly survived his time as Dean: the Joseph Window, the Window of the Four Doctors, the Te Deum Window and the Jesse Window, to name a few. When Bishop Pilkington visited the Cathedral in 1567 he said there were still images which should have been destroyed (by this time Whittingham had been Dean for five years) and, indeed, there are still some which have escaped the iconoclast's hammer to this day. Bishop Hatfield still lies in the choir, resplendent in his mass vestments and the roof bosses in the Nine Altars Chapel still depict the flamboyant figures of the Evangelists. Why, we may ask, did the 'great villain of the Geneva gang' do nothing about them?

Perhaps what focussed the venom of the author of the *Rites of Durham*, and the later antiquaries, so firmly on Whittingham was not so much his structural alterations as his supposed hostility to the cult of St Cuthbert which had been fundamental to the whole ethos of the old Prior and Convent. We are told that he destroyed a statue of the saint which used to stand in the cloister 'to the intent that there should be no memory of that holy man, St Cuthbert'; and Mrs Whittingham burned St Cuthbert's banner in her kitchen fire 'in the notable contempt and disgrace of all ancient and goodly relics'.[15] Though this was controversial stuff, enough to raise the hackles of any red-blooded Dunelmian, it must also be remembered that in

---

14 Marcombe, 'Dean and Chapter of Durham', p. 204.

15 Fowler (ed.), *Rites of Durham*, p. 27.

Dobsons Drie Bobbes, a book about George Dobson, a chorister in the cathedral in the 1560s, St Cuthbert's shrine and some of the 'ancient monuments' connected with it were still being spoken of as something of a tourist attraction (to latter-day pilgrims, perhaps?).[16]

So here we are getting contradictory signals and mixed messages, and we must try to explain why. The reasons for this are almost certainly to do with the personality of the Dean and the circumstances in which he found himself. Whittingham's attitude was certainly not consistent. For example, on the one hand he hated wonder-working relics (such as the banner) which just had to go; yet on the other, he was a lover of music so the organs could stay. Always a careful manager of money it made no sense to destroy those huge stained glass windows, even if their content was offensive. They would have had to be replaced to keep the building watertight ... at huge potential cost. And what about his colleagues in the Chapter ... whose support was needed to implement most of these changes in any case? By 1570 many of the prebendaries were puritans, like the Dean, but an influential Catholic faction lingered on, represented by men such as Thomas Sparke, who saved the bells. The Dean had to respect their wishes, up to a point, and his freedom of action was in this way curtailed. Much of the Dean's life on the Cathedral close, one suspects, revolved around doing deals and negotiating compromises ... and certainly not getting all of his own way all of the time.

If none of this is very surprising in the light of the way in which other Cathedrals worked and operated – and engaged in iconoclasm – the case of Durham has lived on in the popular imagination because eighteenth and nineteenth century antiquarians latched on to it and wrote critically about it. This was the age of the Gothic Revival, when everything medieval was revered and the Protestant tradition was under attack. Little wonder that High Church historians, such as Hutchinson, saw in Dean Whittingham an embodiment of evil ... particularly, perhaps, for his hostility to St Cuthbert. In this climate puritans in general were regarded as 'repulsive, as well as inhuman' and Whittingham, personally, was accused of 'acts of violence and irreligion', which made him 'the mark of public reprehension' and set him beneath 'the most ignorant of savages'.[17] This cultivated man ... 'the most ignorant of savages'? I wonder how Whittingham would have reacted to an article in the *Church Times*, just two weeks ago on

---

16 *Dobsons Drie Bobbes* was first published in 1607. E.A. Horsman's edition (Oxford, 1958) refers to St Cuthbert's shrine on p. 83.

17 Hutchinson, *History of Durham,* vol. 2, p. 188; J.F. Hodgson, 'The Church of Auckland St Andrew', *Archaeologia Aeliana,* New Series, 20 (1899), p. 107.

8 February 2002. It explains how the police were called to keep order in a dispute over the treatment of a redundant church at No Man's Heath, near Tamworth:

> 'A hard core of campaigners has been whipping up hostility by saying that all the graves are going to be dug up and replaced with a cesspit', a diocesan spokesman said on Tuesday ... Warwickshire police kept a low profile, and were praised by the diocese for their sensitive handling of the protest. Mr Williams [Secretary of the Redundant Churches Uses Committee] said on Tuesday: 'In 30 years as a priest, I have never had such an unpleasant day'.[18]

Contemporary incidents such as this are far, far in excess of anything even alleged against Whittingham, and on the basis of church-wrecking activities engaged in by the Church of England today, I find him 'Not Guilty' on the second count.

If the charges of puritanism and unbridled iconoclasm are non-proven, what about the strange circumstances of the 1578 Visitation which sought to get rid of him altogether? Royal Visitations of this type were comparatively rare and the circumstances leading up to it were highly complex, to say the least. Basically, the upshot was that by 1578 a number of powerful people had had enough of the Dean and wanted to be rid of him – though, ironically, the charges levelled against him in the 1578 Visitation were not the same as those (*i.e.*, puritanism and iconoclasm) taken up by posterity. By contrast, the visitors of 1578 were worried about three issues. That Whittingham had presided over a corrupt regime in the Cathedral and had misappropriated funds. That he led an immoral life and was often drunk. That he was not a properly ordained minister and was therefore insufficient for his post. The first two were fairly stock accusations which could be levelled against virtually any senior Tudor churchman. The third was slightly more worrying and turned out to be the issue on which the whole investigation hinged. But why did Whittingham find himself in this position? Who were these powerful individuals who were going to such great lengths to bring him down ... and why?

Whittingham's enemies represented a bizarre and somewhat unholy alliance of three disparate groups or individuals. First, there was what might be termed the clerical interest comprising the new Archbishop of York, Edwin Sandys, and the equally new Bishop of Durham, Richard Barnes. These two had got together to organise a metropolitan visitation of the diocese of Durham from York following Bishop Pilkington's death in 1576. This, of course, was an issue

[18] *Church Times*, 8 February 2002, p. 4.

designed to raise steam at Durham. Indeed, according the *Guinness Book of Records*, the longest running lawsuit is the ongoing one between York and Durham over ecclesiastical jurisdiction, bitterly fought out since the days of Anthony Bek in the thirteenth century. Without a bishop in place, Whittingham took it upon himself to protect the privileges of the see, and when Barnes tried to visit the Cathedral (in the name of the Archbishop of York, not in his own as Bishop of Durham) the Dean turned him away at the Chapter House door on 8 August 1577. The case ramified messily and expensively around the courts of law and, most important of all, Sandys and Barnes felt miffed. According to Whittingham's biographer, they considered it 'a disgrace offered them and such as could not be laid aside without a revenge'.[19]

The second difficulty centred around an individual, Sir Thomas Wilson, Elizabeth's new Secretary of State, who had been a candidate for the Deanery of Durham back in 1563 and had been thwarted by Whittingham's unexpected appointment. Not only did Wilson want to get his own back; he wanted the Deanery for himself. He was supported in this by many courtiers who had seen their ambitions frustrated by the alliance between old Bishop Pilkington and Dean Whittingham in the north during the 1560s and 1570s. This was the great age of fleecing the church, and powerful people expected favourable leases of church lands to be given to them without argument. Pilkington and Whittingham were made of sterner stuff and consistently refused to collude with the diminution of their temporalities. A sort of 'test case' had become the so-called 'Grand Lease' of the Gateshead and Whickham coal mines which Pilkington had consistently refused to hand over to an up-and-coming group of capitalists in Newcastle, the Hostmen. Huge sums of money were potentially bound up with this deal, but it could not be unlocked before the Bishop actually *granted* the lease and the Dean and Chapter *confirmed* it. With Pilkington out of the way after 1576, that left Whittingham as the major obstacle. If Wilson could displace him, the price of his preferment would be the confirmation of the 'Grand Lease' to the Hostmen. Barnes was amongst the most obsequious of Elizabeth's bishops and had already promised, in effect, to grant it.

The third element in this alliance was the wild card, the puritan prebendary of Durham and Master of Sherburn Hospital, Ralph Lever. Although Lever shared many of Whittingham's religious views, there seems to have been personal animosity between them. Whittingham, with his penchant for scholarship, overseas travel and diplomacy, must have been an easy man to get on with, but Lever was precisely the opposite. He was arrogant, opinionated and almost

---

19 'Life of Whittingham', p. 28.

certainly manic-depressive. Because of this clash of personalities, Lever became excluded from the inner ring of puritan prebendaries who ruled the Cathedral during the 1560s and 1570s and who divided up the lion's share of the profits accrued from Chapter leases and entry fines levied on tenants. Especially important during this period were the 'lotteries', divisions of leases amongst the prebendaries made in the expectation that the sitting tenant would buy back the lease from the prebendary in question as an additional guarantee of his position. Because Lever had not done as well as he expected out of all of this he blew the whistle on the Dean. Hence the allegations of mismanagement, and, no doubt, the exposure of some of Whittingham's more personal weaknesses, such as his liking for a drink or two. With the unity and the confidentiality of the Chapter split by the revelations of this mentally unbalanced 'mole', virtually anything could happen.

And it did. To cut a long story short, the combined influence of Sandys, Barnes, Wilson and Lever was sufficient to persuade the Queen to issue a commission for the Visitation of Durham Cathedral on 14 May 1578 under the chairmanship of Henry Hastings, Earl of Huntingdon, Lord President of the Council of the North. Barnes, hardly an impartial source, spoke of cleansing 'that Augean stable, the church of Durham ... whose stink is grievous in the nose of God and of man and which to purge far passeth Hercules' labours'.[20] He was right ... on the last point, at least. The commissioners met for sessions at Durham and York, but before long the whole thing had degenerated into a fiasco. Though most of the charges against the Dean dealt with mismanagement and immorality (where there was, at least, a *grain* of truth), the entire discussion became bogged down on the controversial question of his ordination – whether he was properly ordained by Genevan standards and whether Geneva orders were acceptable in the Church of England in any case. This immediately alienated Ralph Lever who had no problem with the Dean's ordination and wanted his allegations of corruption fully explored.

Over the question of the ordination the commissioners were bitterly divided, Sandys and Barnes being opposed to Whittingham at every juncture; but Huntingdon and Robert Hutton, Dean of York, coming out strongly in his support. There were some unedifying exchanges, especially between Sandys and Hutton, who were old sparring partners from York. When the Archbishop pointed out that the orders of Geneva, which Whittingham claimed, did not accord with those of the Church of England, the following conversation took place:

[20] British Library, Lansdowne MS 25, ff. 161-2.

> Hutton: I dare defend with any Papist in Europe that the orders at Geneva are more agreeing to the word of God than Popish orders.
>
> Sandys: If you defend and like so well of those orders, leave your own orders and take those (and these words he spoke in great anger).
>
> Hutton: No, my Lord, my orders are better than yours, for I was made a minister by the order of the Queen's majesty and laws now established and your Grace a priest after the order of Popery, which order of this realm is better than your Grace's order or any Popish orders.
>
> Sandys: What, dost thou call me a Papist? If I be a Papist then thou art a Puritan ... I am a Bishop, an Archbishop, and that is better than thine.

And the disputes did not end at the council table. That night during dinner the Archbishop refused to eat, drink or speak, until, when the guests had left, he suddenly burst out that he would not be disgraced by the Dean 'or any such churl'. While Hutton adopted an attitude of cynical detachment and Huntingdon desperately attempted to conciliate, Sandys became more and more abusive, saying of Dean Hutton, 'he is a malicious man, puffed with pride at his learning ...' and turning to Mr Dean said, 'What art thou? I am a doctor as well as thou art and as well learned in divinity ... What is thy preaching? But a little heaping up of doctors and poets, little edifying'.[21]

When the last session broke up in disarray, Whittingham, sensing his advantage, went to London to try to get the commission revoked, only to find the Privy Councillors as deeply divided as the commissioners. The whole incident had touched a raw nerve which split the Elizabethan establishment right down the middle. Since the Royal Commission reached no firm conclusion on any of the questions it set itself we must assume, once more, a 'Not Guilty' verdict for the Dean on the third of the great charges levelled against him.

The bitter conflict of 1576-79 seems to have taken its toll on the Dean's health and after a sickness of nine weeks he died on 10 June 1579, aged about 55. He was buried in the Cathedral where his bones still lie, though his monument is long gone. The 'Black Legend' – based on Whittingham's puritanism, his iconoclasm and the events of the 1578 Visitation – must be treated with extreme caution and my 'Not Guilty' verdicts (on each charge) are more a reflection of the Scottish 'Not Proven' than a clear-cut statement of Whittingham's

---

[21] Marcombe, 'Dean and Chapter of Durham', pp. 252-3.

innocence. Obviously he *was* a puritan; he *did* engage in iconoclasm; and he *was* called to account by his enemies in 1578 – but none of that was on a scale to dictate our judgement of him. We might equally remember him for his scholarship; his courage; and his willingness to stand up for the prerogatives of the diocese ... qualities which have placed other Durham *alumni* on pedestals. Whittingham had the misfortune to be unfashionable when much of our local history was being written in the eighteenth and nineteenth centuries, and for that reason we still tend to remember him as 'a great villain of the Geneva gang' rather than the man who brought the standards of the Renaissance to the far north of England. I hope that this talk has at least encouraged a reconsideration and a recognition of a man who is, for me, one of the truly great Deans of Durham.

'The Sacrament it selfe is turned well neare into a theatricall stage play': Liturgical Innovations and Reactions in the 1620s

Brian Crosby

I should like to preface my remarks by pointing out that my subject – 'Liturgical Innovations and Reactions in the 1620s' – was covered in the very first Cathedral Lecture, that of 1969. I cannot claim to remember Canon Turner's precise approach in the Monks' Dormitory on that occasion, but I gather that the reason why his lecture was never published was because, having agreed to give it at relatively short notice, he felt that he had not had time to research it as thoroughly as he would have liked.

When I agreed to re-present the controversy in which prebendaries Peter Smart and John Cosin were the principal antagonists, I thought I was quite well informed about it, but as my preparations continued I became increasingly aware of the breadth and depth of the subject, and how what I shall now present is more a ferreting about in the topsoil than a serious excavation. Where in advance of those preparations I began my title with the quotation, 'a theatricall stage ... especially when the sacraments are admynistred', I now would prefer to replace that quotation with the very similar, 'the Sacrament it selfe is turned well neare into a theatricall stage play'. My reason for wanting to make this change is quite simple – my new choice is from the primary source [Peter Smart's *Sermon*[1]] on which I shall be concentrating, where what I had chosen is not.

As I proceed you may be struck by two thoughts. You may feel that some of the passages I shall quote could have been uttered by a certain clergyman politically active today. You may also feel that what I am describing is nothing more than a low church/high church controversy, the sort of unrest which is caused whenever a new incumbent of a parish changes what had previously been done. To this I would respond, 'Yes, and No!' Where this incident differs is that

1 *A Sermon preached in Durham Cathedral. July 7. 1628.* The Chapter Library, Durham, has three copies: I.VII.87 (used as the source for this lecture) and I.VII.88 were published in 1628, I.VII.85 in 1640. All three give the wrong date, for W.H.D. Longstaffe (ed.), *The Acts of the High Commission Court within the Diocese of Durham* (Surtees Society, 34; Durham, 1858), p. 198 has 27 July. Reference to the Almanac in a contemporary Book of Common Prayer confirms that the 27th was a Sunday.

it occurred relatively early in the history of the Church of England and was of political significance as well.

Although Henry VIII's break with Rome in 1534, and the establishment of the Church in England, was made on political rather than religious grounds, the early sixteenth century saw the culmination of the reaction throughout Europe to the control exercised from Rome by the Church. Men desired the freedom to pursue their scientific observations about the world, the universe in which they lived, and not to be under threat of excommunication, torture and death if their opinions did not meet with the Church's approval.

There was also a growing desire that people should be able to read the Bible for themselves in their own languages; relics and the sale of indulgences had become discredited; statues and prayers through saints were regarded with suspicion; and ceremonial and complicated music sung by trained singers were seen as preventing an individual from communicating directly with God. In contrast, the religious reformers laid emphasis on prayer and penitence and on all the people being able to sing God's praises.

The reformers gained the upper hand in England during the reign of the boy-king Edward VI, but the swing back to Rome under Mary saw many of them flee the country and make Geneva their base. There John Calvin became their leader. Under Elizabeth I the exiles returned. They gained an early victory with the *Act of Uniformity* in 1559. That victory, which took two attempts to get through the Commons and was passed by the Lords with a majority of only one, did not reflect the mood of all the country. Under James I, the reformers tried to gain further ground, but were met with 'No Bishop, no King'.

Calvin's sister is said to have married William Whittingham, who had also sought refuge abroad.[2] Whittingham, a co-translator of the Geneva Bible and the writer of a number of the metrical psalms included in the Sternhold & Hopkins edition of 1562, is important to this lecture's background because he returned to England to become Dean of Durham from 1563 to 1579. In a letter written in 1563 to Cecil, Elizabeth I's secretary, he described the pattern of worship he had introduced in these terms:

[2] C.J. Stranks, *This Sumptuous Church* (London, 1973), p. 44, expressed doubts about this claim. His doubts would appear to be justified in the light of David Marcombe's statement that Whittingham married Katherine Jacqueman (see above, p. 4).

> First in the morning at six of the clock, the grammar school and song schole, with all the servants of the house, resort to prayers in the church; which exercise continueth about half-an-houre. At nyne of the clock we have our ordinary service; and likewise at thre after none. The Wednesdays and Fridays are appointed to a general fast, with prayers and preaching of God's word. The Sundaies and holydays before none we have sermons and at after none the catechisme is expounded.[3]

It was this pattern of worship, with its emphasis on penitence, prayer and preaching being the constituents of praise, with which Smart was familiar. His contentment, however, was shattered by the changes which began to be introduced once Richard Neile had been appointed as Bishop of Durham in 1617.

The influential Neile, who numbered among his protégés Francis White (who became Bishop of Carlisle) and William Laud (later Bishop of London and Archbishop of Canterbury), passed through five bishoprics between 1608 and 1631, when he became Archbishop of York. He had been attracted to the more recent thinking of the Dutch theologian Jacobus Arminius (1560-1609). The result was that Durham House (then the Bishop of Durham's London residence) became very much the meeting-place for those who wished to discuss the new thinking. Probably oversimplifying the differences between Calvin and Arminius, it could be said that where Calvin postulated predestination, that is, a man's fate being pre-determined irrespective of the life he lived, Arminius, like the prophet Ezekiel, advocated that how a man lived could influence his ultimate destiny. Where the original Protestant reaction had endeavoured to free worship of what were considered to be irrelevant distractions, the feeling was now growing that worship had become both monotonous and casual, and that ceremonial dignified worship and uplifted the minds of the people. Unlike the Calvinists, and later the Puritans, who could see only diametrically opposed alternatives, the English Arminians did not consider themselves to be agents of the Pope. They were committed to the Church of England, but wanted it to benefit from the strengths of both traditions.

Neile's succession of domestic chaplains – Augustine Lindsell, Francis Burgoine, Ferdinand Moorcroft, John Cosin and Eleazar Duncon[4] – were understandably men of the same persuasion as himself – and in due course he appointed them all as prebendaries of

---

3 Bodleian Library, Oxford, MS Rawl. D.1364, f. 8.

4 Lindsell, prebendary, appointed 1619; Burgoine, preb., 1617; Duncon, preb., 1628; Moorcroft, preb., 1615; Cosin, bishop's chaplain, 1619, preb., 1624, bishop, 1660.

the cathedral. In sympathy with their thinking was Richard Hunt, who was Dean from 1620 to 1638.

Of Cosin, who had also been one of Neile's chaplains at Rochester, more must be said, for by the time of Smart's outburst against the changes, Cosin was already being regarded with suspicion by the national puritanical element. He was already a Durham prebendary when he was given the responsibility of ensuring that the coronation of Charles I in 1626 was liturgically correct. Its ceremonial had not been appreciated by the Puritans. Cosin had then further incurred the displeasure of the Puritans by preaching in support of bishops at Bishop White's consecration, by successfully defending Richard Montagu from the theological charges against him, and particularly by responding in 1627 to the invitation to compile *A Collection of Private Devotions or The Houres of prayer* for the ladies in attendance on Henrietta Maria, Charles's Roman Catholic queen. This last action resulted in him being investigated by a hostile Parliament. The charges against him, however, he defended successfully and with some ease. Early in 1628 there was further trouble, but he again easily defended himself against the allegation that he had said 'King Charles hath no more power to officiate in the Church, or to excommunicate, then his horse-keeper'. There is also this reference to Cosin in correspondence between Dr Mead of Christ Church and Sir Martin Stuteville, neither of whom had any known Durham connections. On 29 March 1628 Mead wrote:

> Mr. Cosins was so blind at Evensong on Candlemas day that he could not read prayers in the minster with less than 340 candles, whereof 60 he caused to be placed round the high altar. Besides, he caused the picture of our Saviour supported by two angells, to be set in the quire upon Bishop Hatfield's tombe. A great part, if not the most of the evil of our church, at this present is supposed to come from him and those he wholy ruleth, as my Lord of Durham, who admireth him.[5]

Putting it somewhat differently, the conflict between the Puritans and the Arminians was also one of causes of conflict between the Puritans and Charles I. The news of the Durham controversy was one of the final straws that led to the strong puritan element in Parliament trying to proscribe Cosin and all Arminians. The immediate consequence was that Charles dissolved Parliament in 1629 and decided to rule without it. This ultimately led to the overthrow of the monarchy and Charles's execution. That having been said, it is time to turn to the Durham controversy.

---

[5] Longstaffe (ed.), *Acts of High Commission*, pp. 197-8.

It was at Matins on Sunday, 27th July 1628, that Peter Smart, the second-most senior prebendary[6] ascended into the pulpit. He had been appointed a prebendary in 1609, having previously served as Headmaster of the Dean & Chapter's grammar school from 1597. That he should preach was itself something of an unusual event, for it is said that Smart normally preached only about twice a year, and that it was some seven years since his last sermon.[7] His text, which was taken from Psalm 31, was, 'I have hated them that hold of superstitious vanities'.[8]

The sermon itself is usually dismissed in a few words as either a vituperative or a vitriolic attack on his brother prebendaries and on the changes they had introduced into the ordering of worship in the cathedral. Commentators have then also quickly passed over the immediate consequences of the sermon. Instead, they have concentrated on the formal charges made by Smart in 1629 and substantially repeated before Parliament some eleven years later, and prebendary John Cosin's answers to those charges. As something of a change, therefore, the early part of this lecture will be spent unfolding the content of the sermon itself. However, rather than keep returning to the various issues as he did, what he said will be grouped together under a number of points.

His text, as has already been said, was 'I have hated them that hold of superstitious vanities', and it would appear that, unless the congregation then was particularly erudite and could understand his Latin quotations, that he was not so much addressing his remarks to it as to his brother prebendaries.

He prepared his ground by following up his text with the passages, *Be you perfect ... as your heavenly Father is perfect* [p. 2], *Hate the evill, and love the good* [p. 4], *I hate vaine inventions, but thy law doe I love* [p. 4] and *every man is a lyer, and the imaginations of mans heart are onely evill* [p. 2]. Accordingly, he exhorted his hearers to hate their imaginations and inventions, and to obey God's law which forbids idolatry and those vain inventions. He explained that ceremonies were inventions, and asked,

> And what are Ceremonies? are all vain? are all superstitious? God forbid.
>
> Many are tolerable, A few necessary;
>
> Most are ridiculous? And some abominable. [p. 6]

---

[6] He had been collated to the 6th stall in 1609, and had been transferred to the 4th in 1614.

[7] Longstaffe (ed.), *Acts of High Commission*, p. 198, footnote 'a'.

[8] Psalm 31, v. 7 – but it is v. 6 in modern psalters.

Representation of Peter Smart and his cause, 1641
(taken from G.W. Kitchin, *Seven Sages of Durham*
(London, 1911), opposite p. 99)

Ceremonies, he explained, were but the shadows of reality, and Jesus through his death had altered the nature of religion, had altered what was required of man. He explained,

> to preserve the memory of his benefits he [Jesus] ordeined two Sacraments, & left to his Church liberty to make Lawes and Canons. ... But Popes, and papall Prelates, not content with that simplicity which pleased the Apostles, and primitive Church; would needes adde Ceremony to Ceremony, increasing their number *in infinitum.* [p. 117]
>
> ... the originall cause of most of our superstitious Ceremonies, is that Popish opinion; that Christs Church hath yet Priests Sacrifices and Altars,
>
> Whereas in truth Christ was sent of God to be the last priest, which should offer the last Sacrifice, upon the last Altar, that ever the world should have. [p. 8]

This situation, he said, had been recognized by the reformers and in the Prayer Book which had used instead the words, 'Ministers' and 'Communion Table', and this had been the situation at Durham until about 1617. This contention he presented in this fashion:

> For before we had Ministers, as the Scripture calls them, we had Communion tables, we had Sacraments; but now we have Priests, and Sacrifices, and Altars, with much Altar furniture, and many Massing implements. [p. 23]

and he explained that

> ... the Masse comming in brings with it an inundation of Ceremonies, Crosses, and Crucifixes, and Challices, and Images, Copes, and Candlesticks, and Tapers, and Basons, and a thousand such Trinckets, which attend upon the Masse: All which we have seene in this Church since the Communion Table was turned to an Altar. [p. 11]

This relatively brief list was expanded when he said.

> ... if religion consist in Altar-ducking, Cope-wearing, Organ playing, piping and singing.
>
> Crossing of chushions, and kissing of clouts, oft starting up, and squatting downe, nodding of heads, and whirling about, till their noses stand Eastward.
>
> Setting basons on the Altar, Candlesticks and Crucifixes, burning Waxe-candles, in excessive number, when and where there is no use of Lights.

> And that which is worst of all, guilding of Angels, and garnishing of Images, and setting them up aloft ...
>
> *without doubt there is no religion in that Church.* [p. 23]

For these actions Smart derided his fellow prebendaries by saying,

> Ye blinde popish priests understand ye not that by erecting an Altar ye advance it above the body of Christ ... [p. 13]

Offensive though this statement must have been, it was mild compared with this assessment of them and their actions:

> True Christians ever since their Lords death, have left them both Priests and Altars to Iewes and Gentiles.
>
> But the whore of *Babylons* bastardly brood, doting upon their Mothers beauty, that painted Harlot the Church of *Rome*, have laboured to restore her all her robes and jewells againe: especially her looking glasse the Masse, in which she may behold all her bravery. [p. 11]

He went on to say that what the congregation had seen were just outriders, that the return of the Pope was not far behind. He, therefore, advised his hearers to

> ... fly the superstitious furniture of pompous rites, and Papall Pageants, devised onely to astonish simple people, to ravish their eyes, and mindes, and to amaze them with admiration. [p. 8]

All that was needed now, he said, was

> ... the sacrifice of prayer, of praise, & thanksgiving ... [p. 9]

Smart attacked the religion of his day on two fronts, and took the opportunity to pour further scorn on his colleagues:

> ... either your worship is religious, or civill; if it be civill yee are absurd ideots in honouring stocks and stones more then any poore man who is in the image of God ...
>
> If it be religious you are more absurd in preferring the memory of Christs body and blood, before the whole Trinity: seeing you are baptised in the name of Father, and of the Sonne, and of the holy Ghost, and not in the name of Christ alone. [p. 16]

He also considered a number of other matters, and though he again criticised what was happening, he was not so scathing in that criticism. He accepted the use of copes because the Prayer Book allowed the use of a 'decent cope' at Communion, but he condemned those currently being worn because they were far too ornate and decorated with images. He also felt that when copes were worn was illogical – why were they 'put off, and put on ... so often during one service, not onely to pray, but to reade the Epistle and Gospell, and ten commandements at the Altar ...' [p. 18]. Moreover, if they were used then, why were they not also used for the Litany or for the reading of the Psalms and Lessons at Morning and Evening Prayer?

He also wondered why if people reverenced the Communion Table they did not also reverence the Font, especially as 'without Baptisme none can bee saved' [pp. 13 & 15]. It seemed illogical to him that the Font was not in the chancel like the Communion Table, but 'behind the quire dore' [p. 17]. And though he thought that when it was in use the Communion Table should be in the middle and not at the east end of the chancel, and attacked the return to the custom of the officiating Minister standing on the west side [p. 36], he conceded that it did not really matter on which side the officiant stood. Indeed, he was in danger of being humorous when he said that it was a pity it was not a square Table, then the question of sides and ends would not arise! [p. 33]. He also regretted that at the end of a service the congregation was dismissed without a blessing [p. 18].

More hostile because of its language was his observation that ministers were ordained to read and to preach, and not to sing, which 'any lewd Lay-man can doe ... without laying on of Bishops hands, without consecration.' [p. 21]

From what he had said a couple of pages earlier it appears that in making this last remark he was commenting on his own fault-finding question,

> ... why sing they the *Nicene Creed* in a *Cope* at the Altar, the booke [the Prayer Book] appointing it to be said as the Apostles Creed is said, not sung. [p. 19]

At this point it should be mentioned that the role of the Durham minor canons over the centuries has long been uncertain, and I find myself wondering whether they – there were six of them at the time – were singing with the lay clerks and choristers in the canticles and anthems. Whether they were or not in its turn poses further questions of musical importance.

Smart's concern about the Nicene Creed was not confined to the fact that it was being sung, for he also asked,

> Why make they the people to stand up when it is sung ... ? [*ibid.*]

This second question, which may surprise you, reveals what Smart claimed was a change from what was authorized by the Prayer Book. Reference to contemporary Prayer Books reveals that where the rubric enjoined the people to stand for the Apostles' Creed at Matins and Evensong there was no such injunction relating to the Nicene Creed at Communion.

One thing is certain, it was not just the singing of the Creed but the musical content of the services that greatly displeased Smart. In the sermon he asks:

> ... why forbid they the singing of Psalmes in such a tune, as all the people may sing with them, and praise God together, before and after Sermons, as by authority is allowed, and heretofore hath been practised both here and in all reformed churches? [pp. 19-20]

Smart is here objecting that where the congregation used to be able to join in the hymns, which took the form of metrical versions of the Psalms, this was no longer possible because the hymns had been replaced by anthems sung by the choir. He continued,

> How dare they, in stead of Psalmes, appoint Anthems (little better then prophane Ballads some of them) I say, so many Anthems to be sung, which none of the people understand, nor all the singers themselves ...[9] I blame not the singers, most of which mislike these prophane innovations, though they be forced to follow them? ...
>
> Their guides are in fault, blinde guides, members of our Church, ... to whom all men and women are rank puritans and schismaticks to be thrust out and expeld if they refuse to dance after their fantasticall pipe in every idle ceremony. [p. 20]

Although this is to some extent a repetition of the previous paragraph, the scope of his objection has been extended with his use of the expression, 'prophane Ballads'. Anthems may have been unacceptable, but some anthems were more unacceptable than others! In the most unacceptable category were anthems whose texts were not in the Bible or in the Prayer Book or setting of the texts of metrical psalms.

Not named in the Sermon itself, but singled out elsewhere[10] for attack was the anthem known as *The three Kings of Colen*. Cologne has long claimed to be the last resting place of the Wise Men, hence

---

9 *Cf.*, G. Ornsby (ed.), *The Correspondence of John Cosin, Bishop of Durham*, vol. 1 (Surtees Soc., 52; Durham, 1869), pp. 183-4, Item 16, and p. 166, Item 8.

10 Item 9 of *A briefe but true historicall Narration of some notorious Acts and Speeches of Mr. John Cosin*. This publication is added after the *Sermon* in Durham Chapter Library, I.VII.87.

the title of the anthem. Cosin for his part denied introducing it. Indeed, he asserted that because its text was neither scriptural nor from a hymn he had caused the anthem to be cut out of the books that included it for years.[11] Consequently, it is not extant in any music manuscript today, not in Durham or anywhere else. Its text, however, may not be unrelated to this verse preserved in the common-place book of Elias Smyth and said to be then displayed in the principal church in Cologne:

Three kings unto the king of kings 3 gifts did bring,
  Myrrhe, incense, gold, as unto man god king
Three holy gyfts be likewise given by thee
  To Christ, even such as acceptable be.
For Myrrhe bring teares, for Frankincense impart
  Submissive prayers, for gold a pure hart.[12]

Nor was the musical criticism limited to what was being sung, for included in yet another version of the comprehensive picture is:

> And though our Leiturgy be not in Latine, yet order is taken by confusednesse of voices, some squeaking, some blating, some roaring, and thundering with a multitude of melodious instruments that the greatest part of the service, is no better understood, then if it were in Hebrew or Irish.
>
> Nay the Sacrament it selfe is turned well neare into a theatricall stage play ... when mens minds should be occupied about heavenely meditations. [p. 24; *cf.*, *Acts of High Comm.*, p. 235, Ans. 13.ii]
>
> Choristers, and singing-men, and parti-coloured Cope-wearers, *fremunt* they shout and cry, and make most sweet Apollinian harmony. [p. 24]

The reference to 'a multitude of melodious instruments', whilst something of an exaggeration, was not just to the organ and the different sounds it could make, as we shall shortly hear. As for the reference to the theatre, the quotation originally chosen as the title to this lecture was taken not from Smart's sermon but from one of his personal notebooks.[13] Three of these are now in the Bodleian Library, Oxford. In full the passage in the notebook is,

> If the house of God were ever made a theatricall stage for the people to heare and see playes acted therin, the Cath: church of Durha~ is such an one at this tyme, especially when the sacraments are admynistred, wch if St Jerome were now alyve

---

11 Longstaffe (ed.), *Acts of High Commission*, pp. 225-6.

12 Hunter MS 125, p. 133. Smyth was a minor canon from 1628 to 1676.

13 There are several in the Bodleian Library.

> to heare and see, when Mr. Burgoyne, Mr. Cosyn, Smyth, and Leonards in theire Babalonish and pybald vestments are the Actors with theyr glittryng picturs, and histronicall gestures, with all the confused voyces of the singing-men and quoristers with a multitude of melodious instruments, no doubt but Jerome would say, that the wicked spiritt cast out of Saule is entred into Cosyn and his fellow-singers, pipers, ~~tobacconists and drunkards~~ [*sic*] ... [MS Rawl. D.1364, ff. 8-9^{v}]

Suffice it to say at this stage that Burgoine and Cosin were prebendaries, Smith and Leonard minor canons, Smith being the William Smith of Responses' fame.[14]

In the privacy of his notebooks Smart felt able to give full vent to his feelings and to name names, where in his Sermon he felt it was incumbent upon him to be – you may be surprised at my choice of words – more circumspect, more restrained! There, the nearest he felt able to go was:

> Our young *Apollo* repaireth the quire, and sets it out gayly, with strange Babylonish ornaments; the hallowed Priests daunce about the Altar, making pretty sport, and fyne pastimes, with trippings, and turnings, and crossings, and crouchings ... [*Sermon*, p. 24]

and

> This makes me call to remembrance, a strange speech little better then blasphemy, uttered lately by a young man in the presence of his Lord and many learned men.
>
> I had rather goe forty miles to a good service, then two miles to a Sermon.
>
> And what meant he by a good service: his meaning was manifest, where goodly Babylonish robes were worne, imbroydered with images.
>
> Where he might heare a delicate noise of singers, with Shakebuts, and Cornets, and Organs, and if it were possible all kinde of Musicke, used at the dedication of *Nabucho-donosers* golden Image. [p. 22]

Here then we have the other musical instruments to which Smart had alluded, cornetts [about two feet long and looking like recorders] and sackbuts [early trombones]. The '40 miles to a good service' is also mentioned in one of his notebooks, in another unrestrained and somewhat slanderous passage:

---

14 Mark Leonard had been recruited from Windsor on account of the quality of his voice – see British Library, Harleian MS 6583, f. 525.

> ... As for some of our quire-men of Durham more notable drunkards then whom no Cath. church of England hath, they sitt night and day quaffyng and carousing in Alehouses and tavernes ... Silly person among such, renowned John Cosyn delytess Is to be, with his tobacco-pipe, and to chant with them all day long, in comparison of whom he cares not for preachers, for he sayd before his Lord and many others, that he had rather goe 40 myles to a good service then 2 myles to a sermon. (MS Rawl. D.1364, ff. 8-9v)[15]

But again, the temptation to digress must be avoided.

One of Smart's final points was that he said that he could not accept the defence, offered by those who had introduced the practices at Durham, that they had not introduced anything – including the stone altar – that was not in accordance with the worship being offered in the King's chapel. Smart pointed out that the reason why a stone altar had not been introduced into the royal chapel was because the old one, which had been there before the Reformation, had never been removed. He said he felt sure that if had been removed, then it would not have been replaced, as had happened at Durham. In any case, Smart said,

> The King commands us to obey his lawes, not imitate his Chappell contrary to his lawes, which binds Cathedrall Churches as well as the rest ... [p. 33]

Such was Smart's sermon, full of contempt for what he considered to be the ignorant and misguided actions of his younger colleagues. But why did he preach it? Was it the frustrated reaction of someone, who in a minority of one, found himself incapable of arresting the tide that was in full flow? Or was it a calculated action by one who was aware that there were many in Parliament and throughout the country who felt that the Arminians must be suppressed? Did he hope that somehow his voice would be heard, and that the tide would indeed be turned?

Before elaborating on the consequences of Smart's words, it is worth considering to what extent he was exaggerating or even misinterpreting what was happening. The hope that the contemporary Act Book of the Dean & Chapter might include detailed evidence of what was happening is not fulfilled, for the book concerns itself mainly with leases, with appointments, and with the

---

15 *Cf.*, Ornsby (ed.), *Cosin's Correspondence*, vol. 1, p. 185, Item 17.

misdemeanours of the musicians. There are no references to the ordering of the liturgy, and no hint of any disagreement among members of Chapter or indeed of Smart's sermon. However, in an entry made on 9 July 1621 the Act Book does refer to Dean Hunt providing new church plate and taking the decision that morning prayers should in future be held in the choir. The Act Book also records the decision on 15 November the same year to grant the Dean the income from Bywell St Peter's for twenty-one years in return 'for the makeing of the Organes by him lately begunne'. Hunt also replaced the wooden altar with the stone one that can still seen on Good Fridays when the larger superstructure is removed. But it is wrong to attribute any of these actions to Cosin, for they all antedate his appointment in 1624 as a prebendary.

The same, however, cannot be said about 1626. On 29 March that year Chapter was quoted the sum of £112. 5s. 0d. by Francis Hall, a London goldsmith, 'for the furniture of the Alter'. The items listed were 'one Bason ... one Paire of Gilt Potts ... two Candlesticks ...' and 'two Chalices and two Patents', all suitably engraved and having 'cases Made of blacke leather and lined with yellow baies'.[16] Later, on 5 October, it was agreed that three vestments and a white cope should be taken to London 'to be altered and changed into faire and large Copes according to the Canons and Constitutions of the Church of England.' It was actions such as these which were embraced in the Chapter 'Act and ordinance' of 20 July 1628. It referred to 'large summes of money' being expended on 'the repairatons [*sic*] of the Church fabricke, and for the ornaments, utensills and beauty of the same'. The Act also mentioned a system of augments 'for the better Life mainteynance and encouragement of them that daylie performe their due service in the Quire'. As it was made just a week before Smart's outburst, it could have been that last straw.

That there were two cornetts and two sackbuts emerges from payments to named instrumentalists in the three surviving Treasurer's Account books of the 1630s. Although there are no surviving Account Books for the 1620s, a later source – Chapter's corporate reply to Cosin's Visitation Articles of 1665 – dates their introduction between 1624 and 1628, for it includes in the margin this comment about the instruments:

> the Bishop likes them very well having been established in his time when he was a Prebendary heretofore.[17]

---

16 The priced list of items, and the decision on 1 July 1626 that payment should be made, were not minuted until 26 September 1627.

17 Chapter Library, Durham, Hunter MS 11, gathering 83.

Useful evidence also exists in a statement made by Richard Hutchinson, 'Singing-man and Organist of Durham', on 16 March 1628/9.[18] After news of the controversy at Durham had reached London Hutchinson was one of those summoned to appear before Parliament. However, by the time he arrived, Parliament had been dissolved. Nevertheless, his statement was taken down in writing in case the opportunity arose for it to be used. It is a detailed factual statement telling us much about the services both before and after the changes.

> [1.] In former times, the six a clock prayers was read according to the Statutes in a convenient place, so that all Gentlemen and Tradesmen came to it, where they did reade and sing Psalmes, every one understanding another, what was said or sung.
>
> 2. But after a controversie fell betwixt the Deane and M. Cosin, that the one will have it in the Quire, and the other in the older prayer stead, where formerly it hath been used.
>
> 3. It was ordered betwixt them that Prayers should bee sung in the Quire, after the same forme, that we have our ten a clock service from the beginnins [*sic*] unto the ending wirh [*sic*] two Lessons read.
>
> 4. And all the whole members to come in with their gowns and surplices.
>
> 5. But not halfe so many of the Town as did use [to] when prayers were read as formerly have been used.
>
> 6. Then for our ten a clock Service we were commanded to begin with the ten Commandements, and with the Epistle and Gospel, Creed and Anthem, with the Collects after, and so an end, for Munday, Tuesday, Thursday, and Saterday.
>
> 7. On Wednesday, Friday, and Sunday, to begin with the Letany, the ten Commandements, the Epistle and Gospel, Creed.
>
> 8. Then the Sermon, and after an Anthem, the Collect, and an end.
>
> 9. So that before and after Sermons and Lectures we have had of late no Psalmes but all Anthems, and many of the ditties neither in the Bible nor Communion book.
>
> 11. [*sic*] And every Sunday two or three Copes worne.

---

18 To avoid any uncertainty this date is given in both styles.

> 12. And for the order of the Communion, when they come first to the Communion Table, at the entring of the door every one doth make a low congie[19] to the Altar, and so takes their place.
>
> 13. And then the Priest goeth up to the Table, and there he makes a low congie.
>
> 14.Taketh up the bason, and maketh a low congie.
>
> 15. He goeth to all the Communicants, the Quire excepted, and taketh the offerings in that bason; he goeth up to the Table, maketh a congie, and setteth down the bason.
>
> 16. Then he goeth to the end of the Table, and beginneth the exhortation, and goeth on until he commeth at *Lift up your hearts*, that he singeth, and the quire answereth, singing in strange tunes, so far as the Priest and the Answer goeth: then for the rest, one of the Priests reads some part of it at the end of the Table.
>
> 17. And another sitting on his knees at the middle of the Table, and after the prefaces the priest begins, *Therefore with Angels and Archangels*, until he come to the three holies, and then the quire singeth untill the end of that: so in order hee doth administer the Communion.[20]

It has already been pointed out that the decision to move Morning Prayers was taken before Cosin became a prebendary. A more likely objector to the Dean's proposal would have been Smart himself. The 'low congee to the Altar' was not, as Smart himself explains in one of his pamphlets, the act of genuflection, but a gravity-defying inclination of the body forwards so that the head was lower than the seat.[21]

Hutchinson, therefore, supports Smart in testifying to the abundance of ritual, to the wearing of copes, to anthems replacing metrical psalms and to some of those anthems having texts not in the Bible or the Communion Book. Although he makes no comment

---

19 A variant of 'congee', that is, a bow or reverence.

20 A printed 1640s copy of Hutchinson's evidence is added to the Trinity College, Cambridge, copy of P. Smart, *Canterburies Crueltie* (1643); *cf.*, V. Staley (ed.), *Hierugia Anglicana, Documents and Extracts Illustrative of the Ceremonial of the Anglican Church after the Reformation*, 3 vols (London, 1902-4), vol. 2, pp. 226-7.

21 'D. Cosin dishonoured and reviled Christian people in the Church, yet he made low legs to the Altar, so low that his breech was higher than his head, as was proved before the Lords in Parliament.' (P. Smart, *A Short Treatise of Altars* (London, 1641, but written in 1629), p. 14, marginal note; *cf.*, Staley (ed.), *Hierugia Anglicana*, vol. 2, pp. 105-6).

whether the Nicene Creed was said or sung, he clearly states that both the *Sursum Corda* and *Sanctus* were.

What was sung during services is also testified to by a number of witnesses of a different kind. They were not people but were and are the manuscript music books used by the choir and organist at that time. Durham is fortunate still to have twenty-nine music books copied between 1625 and 1640 as well as a number of later replacement copies of books that had worn out. Their contents reveal that Smart and Hutchinson could have complained far more about what was being sung by the choir, for as well as about twenty settings of the Nicene Creed, there are a similar number of settings of *Kyries*, or to be more accurate the Responses to the Ten Commandments. The Creeds were clearly sung by the choir, and not, as Smart implies, just by the officiating Minister. There are also a few settings of the Gospel Sentences, and a few of *Glory be to God on High*, though the latter are not grouped together with other movements of the Communion Service but are found in the anthem books. There are also numerous anthem settings of the Collects. What is not clear is whether they were sung solely as anthems, or whether at times the choir usurped the role of the officiating minister. According to its sub-heading, 'At the Communion', in a Durham MS now in York Minster Library, the anthem, *I will wash my hands in innocency*, was sung during the Administration of the Sacraments.[22] Noticeable by their absence from the manuscripts at Durham are settings of the *Sursum Corda* and *Sanctus*. There is one by John Foster in the York Minster MS, though at the time of Smart's attack he had not even become a chorister.[23].

Moreover, where the sermon limited the scope of its attack to the Communion Service, the music at Matins and Evensong could have been included as well. Certainly, at Christmas, Epiphany, Easter, Ascension Day, Whitsunday, and All Saints' Day the choir sang festal settings of the *Venite* and of the Psalms appointed for the day. As for the 'profane ballads', anthems with non-Biblical or non-Prayer Book texts there are only a few.[24]

---

22 York Minster Library MS M 29 S (the 'Dunnington-Jefferson MS'). The headings in its Table of Contents agree with those of the Peterhouse music MSS, a situation which suggests that the York MS may have been used by Cosin himself. Those headings – Prayer, Penitence, and Praise – would surely have met with Smart's approval.

23 Foster was a Durham chorister from about 1630 until at least 1638, and master of the choristers and organist from Christmas 1660 until his death in April 1677.

24 For example, 'Alack when I look back' (Byrd) and 'Ah helpless wretch' (Mundy).

But it is time to return to the consequences of the sermon. What was to happen quickly did. Those of his colleagues who had been present at that Matins must have been seething at his openly hostile and disparaging attack. It mattered not that he had named no names, his message was loud and clear. Such a confrontation could not be ignored. At 2 p.m. that same afternoon Dean Hunt, and prebendaries Marmaduke Blakeston [Cosin's father-in-law], William James and John Cosin met in the great chamber of the Deanery in the presence of Cuthbert Sisson, notary public. The meeting does not feature in the Dean & Chapter Act Book, for they met not as members of Chapter, but as a sufficient quorum of the local members of the High Commission, the body empowered to deal with ecclesiastical matters. Smart, who was also a member of the commission, was accused of preaching 'a seditious invective sermon, against the decent and allowed ceremonies within the Church of England'. He agreed to hand over his sermon so that it could be transcribed and examined carefully. Far from being repentant, he asserted 'he would justifie every particular thereof.'[25]

There is not time to consider in detail the actions of the next few months which resulted in Smart being bound over under financial recognizance, barred 'from entering the church', and having the income from his prebend sequestered. All this left Smart no little aggrieved, for his colleagues had acted as witnesses, jury and judge. He determined to pursue them in the courts and made four indictments in respect of the innovations they had introduced into the services. At the Assizes, however, Judge Whitlock dismissed the Smart's charges in open court, stating that he himself 'had been in both an eare and an eye witness that all thinges were done in decencie and in order'.[26]

The following year, 1629, Smart re-presented his case, this time before Judge Yelverton, a renowned Puritan. Having pronounced that just as to do less than was commanded, such as not wearing a surplice, was against the law, so too was to do more than was commanded, Yelverton ruled in favour of Smart. Possibly on reflection he felt he had not been sufficiently impartial, for on the following morning he attempted to reconcile the two factions. He told Smart

> That his natur and disposition was to hot, to revengefull, too fierce and violent, and accordinge to his name, *to smart.*

---

[25] Both quotations are from Longstaffe (ed.), *Acts of High Commission*, p. 198.

[26] Ornsby (ed.), *Cosin's Correspondence*, vol. 1, p. 145.

> That his courses against Mr. Cosin and the Church were *truly* unchristian.
>
> ...
>
> That he found Mr. Cosin of a better temper and disposition than Mr. Smart by farr.
>
> ...
>
> That if he had any power with Mr. Smart, he would advise and charge him to cease from these violent and uncharitable courses, which bred nothing but schisme and sin.[27]

All agreed to a reconcilement, but when Smart asked that the proceedings against him at York should be dropped, his colleagues told him that this was now out of their hands. Yelverton then encouraged Cosin and his colleagues to write to York to say that a reconciliation had been effected, adding that this would count in Smart's favour. He also 'stayed the indictments from any further public view or prosecution', and promised to lay the matter before the King and the Bishops of Durham, London and Winchester.

This resulted in the southern province considering the case. Parliament also discussed the matter, and summoned witnesses, among them Richard Hutchinson, as has been heard. Matters proceeded for a while, but then in March 1630 the King, greatly displeased by Parliament's determination to ban Arminianism, dissolved Parliament.

The York High Commission then secured Smart's return, and in August 1630 he was ordered to recant. His refusal to do so led to him being suspended, fined £400, and committed to prison. In September 1630 he was excommunicated, and in November all his livings were sequestered and he was 'degraded from his clerical status'. His protestation in early 1631 that he had been wrongly imprisoned went unheeded, as did the Articles he submitted to Archbishop Harsnett against Cosin, Burgoine, Blakeston, Dean Hunt, Lindsell and James. In prison Smart remained for over eleven years.

While Smart was in prison Charles I increasingly lost control of his country. Aware that the wheel had turned, Smart petitioned Parliament in November 1640, and the case was re-opened. Nicholas Hobson, the veritable doyen of Durham lay clerks – he claimed to be '92. yeares or thereabouts' – travelled to London in to give evidence in

[27] *Ibid.*, vol. 1, p. 157.

support of Smart.[28] The result was something of a foregone conclusion, and Cosin became the first victim of Puritan vengeance, for Parliament was unanimous in its decision to deprive him of all his preferments. In March the following year twenty-one articles of impeachment were exhibited against Cosin, but after five days at the Bar of the House of Lords Smart's counsel told his client openly "'That he was ashamed of him, and could not in conscience plead for him any longer." Whereupon the Lords dismissed Cosin, upon his putting bail for his appearance; but they never sent for him again.' Cosin resumed his duties at Durham and Peterhouse, but, after being ejected from the latter for sending the College plate to the royal mint at York, he deemed it prudent *c.*1644 to withdraw to Paris. But Cosin was destined to see a new day dawn, for in 1660 he returned to Durham as its Bishop.

As for Smart, his preferments were restored to him in January 1641, but he experienced difficulty in getting from Chapter the money that was owed him. Possibly this was not surprising, for Smart continued to be bitterly aggressive, as his *Treatise of Altars* and *Canterburies Crueltie* demonstrate. It cannot be denied, however, that his eleven years of imprisonment and other humiliations gave Smart grounds for being bitter. His restoration, too, proved to be something of a non-event, for the Durham Dean & Chapter's revenue was confiscated in 1642 in retaliation for it siding with the King against Parliament. This was followed in 1645 by the abolition of the Prayer Book, and in 1649 by the abolition of cathedrals as places of worship. Smart retired to his house at Baxter Wood. There he died in about 1652.

Such was the altercation which did not redound to Durham's credit. Sadly, as I said at the beginning, similar words can be still heard today. The observation by Jonathan Swift, Dean of Dublin [*d* 1745], 'We have just enough religion to make us hate, but not enough to make us love one another', is still very true.

---

[28] Hobson's statement is also added to the Trinity College copy of Smart, *Canterburies Crueltie*; *cf.*, Staley, *Hierugia Anglicana*, vol. 2, pp. 225-6. Hobson was mistaken. Even if he had been as old as 20 when he finished as a chorister in March 1580 he would have only been 82 when he died in 1642.

Re-facing or De-facing? The late eighteenth-century re-dressing of the Exterior of Durham Cathedral

Christopher Downs

Introduction

The casual, lay visitor is unlikely to be aware of the extent of weathering and renewal that the exterior of the Cathedral has undergone over its 900-plus years, though they will curse the architect responsible for the ever-present scaffolding spoiling their photographs. The more observant, or trained, eye will realise that a considerable amount of wholesale masonry re-facing work has been carried out over the last couple of centuries, as the nineteenth and twentieth-century masonry still looks relatively crisp, uniform and regular compared to surviving medieval masonry in general. However, I would dare to suggest that only a very keen observer, with a detailed knowledge of historical architectural design, and even then possibly only when 'tipped off', would detect the evidence of the overall dressing-back of the external stonework of the cathedral which was carried out in the late eighteenth century. So is it right to describe this action as a disaster? Would the building look significantly different if it hadn't been done? Would the alternatives have been any better?

Why it was done

Perhaps we should start by considering the condition that the exterior of the building was in by the last quarter of the eighteenth century. The greater part of the building was erected in 1093 to 1133, so would have been at least 600 years old. The thirteenth-century Chapel of Nine Altars would have been standing for over 500 years. The Central Tower, rebuilt in the fifteenth century, would have been relatively young at around 300 years. Centuries of being left out in all weathers!

Despite present-day paranoia, there is no evidence to suggest that rising pollution levels have accelerated the rate of decay of sandstone out of all proportion, and we can therefore infer from the deterioration of the re-facings carried out with new stone over the last 200 years that if left untended the original masonry surfaces would have been in an advanced state of decay.

There seem to be no references to significant expenditure on the external stonework of the church in the surviving documentary records prior to the 1770's, though repair of the roof leadwork appears repeatedly in the century between the Dissolution and the Civil War.[1] After the Restoration in 1660 the immediate concerns were the re-furnishing of the interior, re-glazing of the windows and – again – repair of the roof leadwork, alongside reparation of the 'Ruines of the Deanery and Prebendaryes houses', rebuilding of Prebends' Bridge, and extensive work on the Claustral buildings including rebuilding of the medieval Frater or Petty Canons Hall to form the new Library (1684) and reconstruction of the cloisters themselves (1763-9).[2]

So it seems likely that the stonework had been left to weather and decay for at least 250 years before the 1770's, and possibly had received no significant attention since originally built. We can get some idea of the condition it is likely to have been in by looking at some of the worst areas of eroded stone evident today (Figs. 1 and 2).

Fig. 1: Eroded stonework on the south side of the Choir

---

1 Abstracts of Chapter Minutes, 3 vols (henceforth ACM), vol. 1, Catalogue of Bills, etc. The Abstracts are in the Chapter Library, Durham.

2 Ian Curry, *Sense and Sensitivity: Durham Cathedral and its Architects*, (henceforth S & S), Durham Cathedral Lecture, 1985, p. 5.

Fig. 2: Eroded stones on the south side of the Choir

But for the definitive account of why this action was taken we need look no further than the report of the surveyor and engineer recommending that it be done. This report, dated 29th November 1777, survives in the Cathedral archives and sets out the results of the survey the writer had carried out since being appointed by Chapter on the 20th. Not surprisingly, he makes more than one reference to pressure of time! In his report, he recommends the filling of a rent in the Nave vault to aid further observation, the taking down and rebuilding of the corner pinnacles and end gables of the north and south ends of the Chapel of Nine Altars and of the two major buttresses on its east front, the rebuilding of the gable turrets of the North Transept, the removal of the upper part of the medieval North Porch, renewal of numerous window surrounds and of the parapets and buttresses of the Central Tower, and addition of ragged pinnacles to this tower and pierced parapets to the western towers. All this sets his third recommendation in the context of a wide-ranging programme expected to take a team of forty men eight years and cost £9,000 (the records suggest that the eventual cost was about £15,187).[3]

It is his third recommendation that is of particular interest to us:

> The third great defect I now take the liberty to mention is obvious indeed to every body, and that is, the almost universal decay or wasting condition of the stones on the outside of the whole structure. To prevent the wet entering and lodging in the walls, and thereby bringing on a more speedy dissolution, and to afford all the remedy that can properly be applied on this occasion, it will be necessary to chip or pare off their outsides to the depth of 1, 2 or 3 inches, as may be particularly required, to bring the upright of the wall to a tolerable even or streight surface, at the same time taking out and replacing such stones as are almost totally perished and moulder'd away, and filling up the joynts and beds of the whole with a proper mortar, struck in with the chips or splinters of flints and gallets, as full as it well can be. It would be proper also while the scaffolding is up to fix on the walls the proper lead wall pipes, to convey the rainwater from the various parts of the roofs to the ground. The walls will thus be brought to as perfect a state of repair as they well can be, and may without any considerable expense, resist the ravages of time perhaps for centuries to come.

This describes precisely what was then done, commencing in 1778 and almost certainly complete by the time the eminent architect James Wyatt was invited to advise the Dean and Chapter in 1794/5 and the influential antiquarian John Carter came on the scene at about the same time.[4]

Who was responsible?

At this point it might be as well to digress and reveal who was responsible for this drastic course of action, not least because much confusion appears to have arisen in various narratives despite the clarity of the documentary evidence.[5] Wyatt, who is rightly castigated for the proposal to demolish the Galilee and for the far from historically

---

3 'Record of Works done in and upon the Cathedral Church of Durham, 1700-1857 and 1858-64' (privately printed), p. xxvii.

4 C.J. Stranks, *This Sumptuous Church* (London, 1973), pp. 80-1.

5 Ian Curry, 'Restorations and Repairs to the Fabric of Durham Cathedral 1777 to 1803' (henceforth R & R), in *Medieval Art & Architecture at Durham Cathedral* (1980; British Archeological Association), p. 130, for a fuller account of who has been blamed for what by whom.

authentic re-design of the east front of the Chapel of Nine Altars, has sometimes been blamed unjustly both for the loss of the medieval North Porch and for the chiselling-off of the external stonework. More recent accounts have implicated the Durham architect George Nicholson, who was both 'Clerk of Works' and 'College Architect' during the period in question.

There is some justice in this, in that he was clearly the executive architect for the works, but the report from which I have just read is not by him. He was one of two people who assisted its author in carrying out the survey, and the final recommendation of the report makes his part clear:

> I must now conclude by expressing my wishes that the Chapter would be pleased to order Mr. Nicholson or some proper person, to take the necessary measures, and draw out from a scale of 20 feet to an inch, correct elevations of the 4 sides of the Cathedral, to correspond exactly with its plan to be correctly drawn from the same scale. The whole will serve as canvass to paint or mark out any necessary alterations the Chapter may judge proper to order in the elevations of the turrets or any other parts of the building.

These drawings by Nicholson formed the basis for the engravings published in Hutchinson.[6]

The signature on this report[7] is that of the Newcastle surveyor and engineer John Wooler, who had been engaged on coastal survey work for the Lord Crewe Charity Trustees in north Northumberland, acted for Newcastle Corporation when the medieval Tyne Bridge (of which the Dean & Chapter owned the Gateshead half) was swept away in the great flood of 1771 and had produced the plans for the new market place in South Shields for the Dean & Chapter in 1768.[8]

The minutes of the Great Chapter of 20th November 1777 record:[9]

> Agreed that Mr. Wooler be Employed to Survey the Church, and to make an Estimate of the Expenses of Repairing and Beautifying it.

It is apparent that John Wooler continued to serve as occasional consultant – in 1779 he prepared a 'Memorial concerning the repairs

6 William Hutchinson, *History of Durham* (1st edit., London, 1787). The plates are omitted from subsequent editions.

7 John Wooler, Unpublished report, 29th November 1777. This and other unpublished reports are filed as Additional MSS in the Chapter Library.

8 ACM, vol. 2, p. 551 (for 28 Sept. 1768).

9 ACM, vol. 2, p. 582.

proposed to be done to the north end of the part called the Nine Altars in the Cathedral of Durham',[10] which is, in effect, a specification for the rebuilding of the north gable and flanking turrets of which most, if not all, appears to have been done. Unfortunately, the drawings to which he refers do not survive, and it is not possible to tell whether it was he or Nicholson who was responsible for the detailed design – though Nicholson is perhaps the most likely as he was a capable designer in his own right, as attested by his elegant design for Prebends' Bridge, built 1772-5.[11]

In 1782 Chapter paid Wooler thirty guineas 'for his trouble in viewing and reporting the state of the church'.[12] The amount as well as the wording of the minute clearly indicates that he was not involved in the day-to-day implementation and supervision of the works.

What were the alternatives, and what did others think?

For the purposes of this discourse I have labelled the chiselling-off of the surface of the stone – with deliberate ambiguity – 'de-facing', as it involved total removal of the original external surface. Three other options would have been available at the time, two of which were in due course adopted by subsequent architects:

Re-facing, by which I mean the complete replacement of the stones forming the outer face of the wall, was adopted by Wooler himself in the north gable of the Nine altars, by Wyatt in the upper parts of the East front of the Nine Altars and by succeeding architects (including Ignatius Bonomi, Thomas Jackson and George Pickering) in the re-facings of the south side of the Cathedral from 1827 to around 1850.[13]

Cement rendering – the application of a specially formulated mortar to simulate stone – was adopted by William Atkinson in the aborted attempt to restore the Central Tower from 1806 to 1808, his appointment being terminated when the effect began to become apparent.[14]

Thirdly, but perhaps only applicable to less seriously eroded areas, there is the method adopted for virtually all the repairs carried out in the last 150 years, involving the retention (without paring-off) of as

[10] John Wooler, 'Memorial concerning the repairs proposed to be done to the north end of the part called the Nine altars in the Cathedral of Durham'. Unpublished report, Feb. 1779.

[11] S & S, p. 7.

[12] ACM, vol. 2, p. 595 (for 20 July).

[13] S & S, pp. 17, 18 and 22.

[14] ACM, vol. 2, p. 681a (for 20/21 November 1808).

much of the original stonework as possible, with new replacement stones inserted where necessary to ensure the continued well-being of the structure and preservation of the design as it now stands.

In considering the virtues and drawbacks of these options it is perhaps instructive – and certainly amusing – to read what successive architects and other writers said about the work of their contemporaries and predecessors:

The historian William Hutchinson, writing in 1787, described the repairs and embellishments then in progress, but seems more concerned with the changes in the design being implemented as part of the overall programme than with the effect of the chiselling-off. He notes:

> This [north] front is under repair, the stones being all chissled over, and the decayed parts restored; the towers will receive new decorations, very different from the ancient ones, and the niches be supplied with new sculptures.
>
> As the proposed changes will effectually remove from the traveller's eye the ancient appearance of this edifice, it was thought expedient to present the public with a representation of the church in the state it was before the repairs began; and notwithstanding the elegance of the present design, it is apprehended that some of the ornaments might have been chosen with greater propriety.[15]

John Carter was more forthright in his condemnations, but his attacks were focused more upon Wyatt's proposals and the work put in hand after 1795 than upon what had gone before.[16]

William Atkinson, in his 'Observation on Repairing and Restoring Durham Cathedral' dated 1804,[17] was more specific:

> It is an object of the greatest importance that its character should be preserved and that the repairs should be done in the most substantial manner; the plan that has been pursued for several years past (in facing & cutting straight the surface of the

15 Hutchinson, *History of Durham*, pp. 63 and 226.

16 For instance: John Carter, *The Gentleman's Magazine* (1802), pt I, pp. 229-31.

17 William Atkinson, *Observation on Repairing and Restoring Durham Cathedral*, 1804. Unpublished report.

> old walls) has been highly injurious to the Building. Besides reducing in size the small parts of buttresses, pillars, & tracery work on the walls – in many instances these must inevitably be cut away or disfigured, and consequently the character of beauty lost. But this is not the greatest mischief that has been done. An old stone new faced seldom stands the weather. In cutting the walls the face of those stones that have stood for ages have been cut away to be made straight with the mutilated parts so that the walls are daily decreasing in thickness and strength.

However, his alternative remedies were not without their drawbacks:

> Perhaps some kind of varnish might be used to preserve the stone in this age for Chemical inquiry. I should think this subject well worth the attention of those gentlemen who make Chemistry their study. I am of opinion that a varnish made of oil and wax would be of great service.
>
> In restoring the Great Tower or any other part of the walls the stones that are perfect, with their original face, should remain & if there should be moss upon them care should be taken not to remove it. Where the stone is very much decayed to a considerable depth, it should be replaced with new, but in general the mutilated parts may be brought out to a proper face with Parker's cement. The old stones should be carefully wet when the cement is laid on, and holes may be drilled to give a stronger tie. This cement is particularly useful in restoring ornaments & mouldings & at a considerable less expense than cutting them in stone. It is nearly the colour of the moss upon the Tower. Stones seldom decay after they once take a moss. From its spongy and fibrous texture it is a good nonconductor of cold & by that means preserves the stone from frost. But what is of still greater importance, its brown tint adds highly to the sublimity of the building – "in buildings when the highest degree of the sublime is intended, the materials and ornaments ought neither to be white nor green, nor yellow, nor blue, nor a pale red, nor spotted but of sad & fuscous colours, as black, or brown, or deep purple & the like." Burke on the Sublime & Beautiful, where new stones are put in they ought to be coloured to suit the old. By following this plan the Tower will be preserved in its original character & a considerable sum saved on the works.

As already mentioned, Atkinson's rendering of the tower was stopped and most of it was eventually removed in George Gilbert Scott's restoration of the 1860s, but it appears that some survived long enough for W.D. Caröe to observe in his 1913 report:

> The southern of the two Lantern lights facing west has been restored in some form of cement, probably Tabary's. New crockets have been cut in the material, and stone joints indicated by drawing trowel lines across it. The whole effect is unsightly in colour and plastic execution.[18]

The effect was perhaps more successful on buildings of a more domestic scale – Nos. 9 and 12 The College having been faced with the same material, presumably also by Atkinson in the early years of the nineteenth century.[19]

Caröe was also rather rude about the re-pointing that had been done in the past – presumably much of it the result of Wooler's recommendation that the joints be filled 'as full as it well can be':

> The general appearance of the fabric has suffered largely – almost over its whole area of surface – from injudicious pointing better known as "slobbering." This consists of spreading mortar or cement, not only into the open joints, but over part of the adjoining stone surface. Whilst most destructive in effect, this is deleterious to the stone, and more especially so if cement is used. ... In good pointing the old mortar should be deeply raked out and the new kept well back from the surface, no part of which it should cover.[20]

The legacy:

So, what are the implications for us of what John Wooler instigated? None of the drawings that survive from the late eighteenth century are detailed enough to indicate what changes arose specifically from the de-facing as opposed to the 'beautification' elements of the programme. However, we can see clear evidence of what was done by close examination of the building itself – firstly, the relationship between the internal corners created by the projecting buttresses (Fig. 3), and secondly the 'tide-mark' visible on the north side of the church – particularly in the corner between the North Transept and the North aisle of the Nave. Here, the soil of the graveyard swept right up against

18 W.D. Caröe, *Report on Durham Cathedral* (London, 1913), p. 21. Copy no. 12 in Chapter Library.

19 S & S, p. 16.

20 Caröe, *Report on Durham Cathedral*, p. 27.

the building at the time the work was done, so the masons stopped at what was then ground level. Subsequent excavation down to the original level to form the wide trench along the north side of the cathedral has revealed the original profiles at the base of the wall arcading (Fig. 4).

Fig. 3: Joint lines indicating extent of chiselling off

Fig.4: The 'tide-mark' where the chiselling stopped at former ground level

In structural terms, the removal of 2, 3 or even 4 inches from one face of a wall some 6 feet thick may not sound significant – even when aware of Billings' calculation that the weight of stone removed (though probably ignoring what had already been lost by erosion) amounted to some 1,100 tons.[21] But it is as well to remember that the Norman masonry consists of two skins of facing stone, varying in thickness but probably around 9 to 12 inches thick on average, with a lime concrete 'plum pudding' forming the core in between. The wall cores of the cathedral church are generally very solid but will not withstand prolonged saturation, so Wooler's concern over dampness in the masonry is well placed.

---

[21] R.W. Billings, *Architectural Illustrations and Description of the Cathedral Church at Durham* (London, 1843), p. 13.

However, the thinning of the outer face means that it is less able to support itself and becomes more of a surface facing on the core. This leaves it prone to failure by detachment from the core work behind, and there has been at least one instance of this happening over the last twenty years, on the east face of the North-West Tower.

More serious is the effect on the thin but boldly projecting buttresses of the East Front, where the removal of 4 inches from each face reduced them from 4 feet 4 inches to 3 feet 8 inches, leaving them more likely to shear under load – though it has to be said that there is no significant evidence of this having happened.

These structural concerns are, however, relatively minor. The main reasons for condemning Wooler's strategy are on grounds of historical authenticity and aesthetics. In removing the external surface of the stonework all the original historic detailing of the building has been compromised. We do not know how much of the architectural moulding work, if any, was copied accurately, but the likelihood is that it was at the very least simplified and at worst either falsified or simply removed altogether. Compare, for instance, the re-faced triforium window recesses on the south side of the Choir (Fig. 5) with those on the de-faced North side (Fig. 6).

Of course, the same risk attends on the alternative strategy of wholesale re-facing with new stone and in the case of these triforium windows we are left in doubt as to whether any of them are historically accurate. It is interesting to note that it was the changes of design attendant on the rebuilding/re-facing elements of the repair programme that attracted criticism at the time.

In terms of aesthetics, we know that there is a likelihood of simplification and modification of the detailing to ease the mason's task, and the possibility that 'improved' designs more to eighteenth-century taste were substituted for the barbarous 'Gothic' or 'Saxon' originals, in the small details just as in the more substantial 'beautifications'. We also know that the various shaftings have been significantly emasculated by reduction of their diameter, with an inevitable change in their proportions relative to the panels of plain walling, the form of the arcade recesses, etc., and an overall flattening of the architectural effect.[22]

[22] R & R, p. 135.

Fig. 5: Restored triforium window on the south side on the church

Fig. 6: Triforium window on the north side of the Choir

We are also left in something of a dilemma of conservation philosophy when it comes to renewal of eroded stone in the areas that were chiselled back. Two alternative responses are illustrated in the windows in the north wall of the North Transept – the aisle window surround (Fig. 7) has been set to the line that the restoring architect thought must have been the original wall plane before the de-facing. The restoration of the main north window, by contrast, has accepted the wall face as received from the hand of the past, however wrong that hand might have been (Fig. 8).

Fig. 7: Renewed surround to west window of North Transept aisle

Fig. 8: Repaired surround to main west window of North Transept

Conclusion:

John Wooler's recommendation to Chapter was probably considered a practical, economical and uncontroversial solution to the problem presented by the eroded masonry of the exterior of the cathedral. Contemporary commentators appear to have been much more concerned about the more deliberate changes to the design of specific elements of the building. However, other architects in the generations that followed were more critical, even though in some cases their own proposals proved no more satisfactory in the long run. In structural terms the effect was unfortunate but not catastrophic. In historical and aesthetic terms the result can only be described as a de-facing in every sense, and – yes – one of the great disasters to have befallen Durham Cathedral.

Beetles in the Holes and Crevices: the Cathedral and reform, 1820-1840

Anne Orde

The last of this series of talks on conflict and disaster in Durham is not so much about controversy within the Chapter as controversy about the cathedral itself and its clergy.

In the years after the battle of Waterloo demand in England for reform grew ever more powerful and widespread. There was a real change of consciousness. Structures and practices that had not been questioned a generation earlier by any except a few radicals now were seen as abuses requiring change. On the political front, the movement led to the first measure of parliamentary reform in the Act of 1832. The Church of England was affected too. Attacks mounted against pluralism and non-residence among the clergy, against sinecures and the politicisation of the bench of bishops. Tithes and church rates were further targets. The position of cathedral establishments also was a subject of attack and argument, and this is what I want to talk about.

The see of Durham was the second richest in the country, coming close after Canterbury, and the cathedral was by quite a long way the richest of all.[1] Moreover, both bishop and cathedral were getting richer. The cathedral had always been well endowed, having been given by Henry VIII almost all of the property of the dissolved priory. Now it was benefiting from the expansion of mining and industry on land that it owned on Tyneside and Wearside, in the part of the county east and south of Durham, and in Weardale. Colliery owners were willing to pay ever-rising fines (that is, lump sums) for leases and rights on such lands; dues on minerals rose with production. To take just a couple of examples among many: in 1768 John Tempest paid £1,100 for renewing the lease of Rainton colliery; in 1805 the fine was £2,500; in 1814 the Dean and Chapter asked for £27,000, and five years later settled with Lord Londonderry for £40,000. The income from Wallsend colliery rose from £616 in 1791 to £2,039 in

[1] *Report of the Commissioners appointed by His Majesty to inquire into the Ecclesiastical Revenues of England and Wales,* Parliamentary Papers, 1835, vol. 22. Average income over three years ending 1831: Sees: Canterbury £22,216; Durham £21,991; London £15,133; Winchester £12,107. Cathedrals: Durham £35,071; Oxford £25,899; Winchester £15,573; Exeter £10,438.

1810 and £3,815 in 1822.[2] Overall the corporate income of the cathedral more than doubled between 1800 and 1830, and expenditure only came to about half of income.[3]

Surplus revenues were divided between the Dean and the twelve prebendaries in an annual dividend, the Dean having a double share.[4] In addition each stall had income from property annexed to it. This was an odd arrangement, unlike the other cathedrals of the new, Henrician foundation. When Henry VIII refounded the cathedral, some lands, known as corps, were allocated to the deanery and individual stalls.[5] The values were originally more or less equal (the dean's a double share), and remained fairly close together until the eighteenth century; but by 1728 the 11th stall got nearly half as much again as the others, and was known as the 'golden stall'.[6] Thereafter the revenues of the different stalls from their corps diverged quite widely, until in the 1830s the 11th stall got three times as much as the 5th, and five times as much as the 9th, which was the poorest.[7] How this came about is not clear. The answer must lie in relative changes in the value of the lands annexed. It is not due directly to coal, since the coal revenues were received corporately. Unfortunately the stall rentals and accounts are not full and continuous enough to provide the necessary detail – those of the 11th stall are the scantiest of the lot – and only some of the payments seem to have gone through the admirably full corporate books, so I have not been able to document it. The dividend from the corporate surplus was the major part of the deans' and canons' incomes, but in some years the richer stalls' corps provided almost half their total. The result of these differences was that prebendaries tended to move

---

2 Durham Chapter Muniments (henceforth DCM), Estate Vols. Contract Book, 1734-1829; Christine E. Hickey, 'John Buddle, 1778-1843, agent and entrepreneur in the North-East coal trade' (M.Litt. thesis, Durham, 1978), pp. 131-6; Alan Heesom, *The Founding of the University of Durham*, Cathedral Lecture, 1982. The Wallsend figures are in DCM Audit Books.

3 Pat Mussett, *Estates and Money at Durham Cathedral 1660-1985*, Cathedral Lecture, 1988; DCM Audit books, Treasurer's charge: 1800 £15,389; 1830 £35,083.

4 Dean's income: 1762, £2,300; 1805, £5,960; 1830, £7,429; average prebendal income: 1762, £700; 1805, £1,770; 1820, £1,921. DCM Audit books; W.B. Maynard, 'The ecclesiastical administration of the archdeaconry of Durham 1774-1856' (Ph.D. thesis, Durham, 1975), pp. 17-18.

5 J. Meade Falkner (ed.), *The Statutes of the Cathedral Church of Durham* (Surtees Society, 43; Durham, 1929), p. 120.

6 DCM, List of Deanery and Prebendal Rentals and Accounts, 1980, appendix; Browne Willis, *A Survey of the Cathedrals of York, Durham ...* (London, 1727), vol. 1, p. 273.

7 *Report of the Commissioners*, 1835: Dean £4,422, 1st stall £925, 2nd £1,000, 3rd £574, 4th £618, 5th £522, 6th £588, 7th £811, 8th £697, 9th £315, 10th £1,183, 11th £1,587, 12th £1,020.

up the scale as vacancies occurred. To take just a couple of examples, Thomas Burgess started in the 9th stall in 1791, moved a year later to the richer 6th stall, and finally in 1820 to the still richer 2nd. John Bird Sumner likewise started in the 9th stall in 1820, moved in 1826 to the 5th stall, and a year later to the 2nd, which he held for twenty years.[8]

The duties of the Dean and canons were not onerous. They were supposed to reside for three months in each year, two canons in residence at a time. When in residence they had to attend the daily services and to preach in turn (there was one sermon a week, at matins on Sundays, and one on the five 'state' days, 30 January, Ascension Day, 29 May, the King's accession, and 5 November). Each had a house, and got an allowance for the time they resided and an extra allowance for the three weeks that was called 'hospitality residence', when the canon concerned was obliged to exercise hospitality, entertaining local notables and the cathedral staff, bedesmen and choir men. There was a cook, who moved from house to house doing the hospitality residence catering.[9] There were eight minor canons, who actually conducted the cathedral services. They were appointed and paid by the Dean and Chapter. Most of them had livings in or near Durham. Archdeacon Thorp described them in 1835 as 'a most useful and meritorious class of incumbent'.[10]

We should not suppose that the deans and canons had no other occupations or sources of income. Of the 25 men who held the dignities between 1820 and 1840, only two had no other position. Several of them were bishops. The Hon. James Cornwallis was dean from 1794 to 1824, for the whole of which time he was Bishop of Lichfield. Thomas Burgess, who as we saw held three stalls in succession from 1791 to 1825, was from 1803 Bishop of St David's. He resigned his stall on being translated to Salisbury in 1825. John Banks Jenkinson succeeded Burgess both in the 2nd stall and at St David's. He became Dean of Durham in 1827 and continued as both dean and bishop until his death in 1840. Jenkinson was followed in the 2nd stall by John Bird Sumner, who was Bishop of Chester from 1828 to 1848, but gave up his stall when he became Archbishop of Canterbury. Robert Gray held the 7th stall from 1804 to 1834,

---

8 Pat Mussett, *List of Deans and Major Canons of Durham 1541-1900* (Durham, 1974).

9 Pat Mussett, 'Hospitality residence at Durham Cathedral', in *Transactions of the Architectural and Archaeological Society of Northumberland and Durham,* NS 6 (1982).

10 Thorp evidence to Commission on Ecclesiastical Duties and Revenues, 1835. Durham University Library (henceforth DUL), Thorp Correspondence, No. 653.

combining it for the last seven years with the see of Bristol.[11] There was one other bishop, Henry Phillpotts. He presents a notable case, and I'll come back to him a little later.

Of the two bishop-deans, Cornwallis was not in Durham at all in the last seven or eight years of his life: he doesn't seem to have left much mark on Lichfield either. Jenkinson, on the other hand, was regular in residence and effective in action, both in his diocese and in Durham. Of the bishop-prebendaries, Sumner resided regularly, Burgess and Gray did not. Both Sumner and Burgess were active in their dioceses. Burgess founded St David's College at Lampeter for the education of poor Welsh clergy, encouraged the use of the Welsh language, and fostered education in general.

The majority of the prebendaries in this period held livings, some in the diocese, some elsewhere. Three of those with livings in the diocese were archdeacons as well – Reynald Bouyer, Richard Prosser, and Charles Thorp. To take some examples, a rather extreme case was the Hon. Francis Egerton. He held the 4th stall from 1786 to 1829, and for most of the time he was rector of two parishes in Shropshire, where he never resided. Egerton went to live in Paris in 1802, and was only seen in Durham once after that. He had some of the instincts of a scholar, and left his papers to the British Museum and a substantial sum of money to the Chapter Library; but he was, to put it mildly, eccentric, keeping numbers of dogs and cats which he dressed up in human clothes, and shooting at captive rabbits and pigeons in his Paris garden.[12] Among those with livings in the diocese were Lord Barrington, who was rector of Sedgefield, William Gilly, who was vicar of Norham, and Robert Gray who was rector of Bishopwearmouth for twenty years before going to Bristol as bishop. His successor at Bishopwearmouth and in the 5th stall from 1827 to 1848 was the Hon. Gerald Valerian Wellesley, brother of the Duke of Wellington. He was also a canon of St Paul's, rector of St Luke's Chelsea, and a royal chaplain. Wellesley did his residence at Durham regularly, but did not reside much at Bishopwearmouth, having a licence from the bishop for twelve years. We do not find him labouring among a sick and frightened flock in the cholera outbreak of 1831, as his neighbour the rector of Sunderland did, earning the lasting gratitude of the town. One hopes that Wellesley's three curates laboured, but he was not there.[13]

---

11 Mussett, *List of Deans and Major Canons.*

12 DCM Audit Book VIII; William Fordyce, *History and Antiquities of the County Palatine of Durham,* (Newcastle upon Tyne, 1857), vol. 1, pp. 255-6; Bernard Falk, *The Bridgewater Millions* (London, 1942), pp. 185-218.

13 Mussett, *Deans and Canons*; Maynard, 'Archdeaconry of Durham', p. 443.

This, I suggest, is not an edifying picture. Here is a group of men paying themselves large incomes, up to ten times the median income of a beneficed clergyman at the time, in return for doing very little. Those who held other positions as well were being paid for them too. This was indeed a period when great discrepancies of wealth were taken for granted, and the upper classes (from which many though not all of these men were drawn) did not expect to work for their living. Sinecures in government posts were common. Cathedral dignities did not involve the cure of souls, so that holding one with a bishopric or benefice was strictly speaking not pluralism. Some people thought, as we shall see shortly, that it was positively a good thing that a cathedral dignitary should hold a benefice and be in touch with ordinary church life. One of the justifications put forward for cathedral sinecures was that they gave rewards for scholarship. This was not a distinguished period for Anglican theological writing, but Durham did not do badly for scholarship in general. Bishop William Van Mildert had been Regius Professor of Divinity at Oxford and published a ten-volume edition of the works of an early eighteenth-century divine, Daniel Waterland, as well as a good many sermons. Of the canons Thomas Gaisford, Regius Professor of Greek at Oxford, edited classical texts; William Gilly wrote several books on the Waldensians; Thomas Gisborne wrote on philosophy and natural theology, George Townsend works on church history and the Bible. William Darnell was an antiquarian and edited texts; and even Egerton founded a series of studies on the power, wisdom and goodness of God as manifested in the Creation. Thinking about the usefulness of an institution was not a thing people did much in the eighteenth century, and it was many years since anyone had actually asked what cathedral establishments were for. The canons of Durham were not, I imagine, unusually greedy men. I have little doubt that they were complacent men. I know of no evidence that it crossed the minds of most of them to think whether they might be doing more for their money. But times were changing, and in the early 1830s these questions were being put.

But before I come to these questions I will return to Henry Phillpotts. He presents, as I said, a notable case, partly because of his personality and behaviour and partly because of the changing times. Phillpotts was the son of a Herefordshire gentleman. He married a niece of Lord Eldon's wife (Eldon was a Newcastle man, a Tory lawyer, Lord Chancellor in the 1820s). Phillpotts's first benefice was near Bath, where he did not reside. He came north in 1805, to the livings of Stainton le Street and Bishop Middleham, and then Gateshead, becoming a chaplain to Bishop Shute Barrington, and a prebendary in 1809, holding first the 9th and then the 2nd stall. He resigned the stall on being given the living of Stanhope. Stanhope was the second richest living in the whole of England.[14] The revenues were derived from the rector's share of the rent on lead mined in the parish, which was booming at the time. From £315 for most of the eighteenth century the sum rose to £1,500 in 1799. In 1820 the London Lead Company offered Phillpotts £3,000 a year: he asked for £5,000 but eventually settled for £4,500.[15] Phillpotts had the rectory rebuilt by Ignatius Bonomi, which suggests that he thought of living there; but he also got licences from the bishop not to reside. In 1828 he was appointed Dean of Chester; he was offered the bishopric of Clogher but declined; and then in 1830 he was made Bishop of Exeter.

This last appointment caused controversy, the like of which would probably not have arisen even fifteen years earlier. Phillpotts was well known as a controversialist, and the bishopric was widely regarded as a reward for his change of mind from being a vocal opponent of Catholic emancipation to support of the government in passing the measure in 1829. He had fourteen children, and said that he could not afford to go to Exeter (one of the poorer sees) unless he could continue to hold Stanhope in commendam – the move would actually have meant a drop in income and considerably more expense. The timing was perhaps rather bad luck on Phillpotts. Three of his recent predecessors at Stanhope had held the living in commendam while being bishops; three of his recent predecessors at Exeter had held livings elsewhere at the same time. But now a row broke out; a petition was got up at Stanhope demanding a resident incumbent; and there was a change of government. The new reforming Whig government led by Earl Grey refused to issue the instrument allowing the commendam, but acknowledged that Phillpotts had been given a promise and undertook to compensate him with the first available suitable Crown appointment that did not involve the cure of souls.[16] The problem was solved by a swap at Durham. William Darnell moved to Stanhope and Phillpotts took Darnell's stall, the 6th. Phillpotts's biographer says that he then performed his duties at Durham regularly. This is not true. He immediately got dispensations from residence, twice for three years at a time, in 1837 for life. He did appear in Durham occasionally, but not often. Phillpotts was an active bishop, known as a disciplinarian and given to litigation. He

---

14 *Report of the Commissioners*, 1835.

15 Maynard, 'Archdeaconry of Durham', pp. 121, 137-9.

16 *Parliamentary Debates*, 3rd series, vol. 1, cols 1187-8, 15 Dec. 1830; Stanhope petition, Fordyce, *History of Durham*, vol. 1, p. 651; Van Mildert to Thorp, 7, 11 and 13 Dec. 1830, Durham Chapter Library, Van Mildert Letters; Van Mildert to Grey, 11, 21, 23, 30 Dec.; Grey to Van Mildert, 22 Dec., DUL, Grey Papers, GRE/B12/10/ 1-5; Phillpotts to Grey, 13, 22, 23 Dec.; Grey to Phillpotts, 13, 24 Dec., Grey Papers, GRE/B14/4/1-5.

wrote on political and church affairs, and spoke often in the House of Lords, opposing the Reform Bill and almost every measure aiming at reform of the Church by the state. He occasioned the famous Gorham case in 1847 by refusing to institute a clergyman whose views on infant baptism were questionable.[17] I have conceived a considerable dislike of Phillpotts, so I must stress that in many ways he was a reforming bishop, who did a good deal to improve residence among the clergy of his diocese, raising the proportion by 70% in ten years.[18]

Phillpotts had made himself notorious in Durham and nationally in the early 1820s by embroiling himself in political controversy, publishing pamphlets in which he accused the local MP, Radical Jack Lambton, and the Whig leader Earl Grey, of inciting the lower orders to sedition. He denounced critics in language which the *Edinburgh Review* described as 'insolent and coarse', characterising one essayist as 'one whose abilities, if accompanied by correspondent elevation of mind, adorned by candour, and directed by wisdom, would enable him to confer lasting benefits on his country and his kind, and even debased, as they too often are, by the coarsest mixture of prejudice and passion, perverted by party-feeling, and abused to the worst purposes of wanton sophistication or wilful injustice, they still render one involuntary service, by the warning they hold out, that intellectual endowments, however great, will never make their profession honourable, without those nobler qualities, which alone can give lustre to eloquence, and dignity to talent'.[19] After one of these attacks Lord Grey described the Durham clergy as animals, and asked: 'What was to be thought of professed followers of Christ shooting forth their poisoned arrows into the world, ignorant and careless where they might hit, so that their malignity was justified?'[20]

One feature of these controversies was the treatment accorded to Queen Caroline, the estranged wife of George IV, whose cause the Whigs took up as a stick to beat the government with. She died in August 1821. She had been kept away from George IV's coronation a year earlier, but she was still his wife, and by custom bells should have been tolled at her death. They were so tolled over most of the country, but in Durham they were silent. The next issue of the *Durham Chronicle*, a recently founded Whig newspaper supported by Lambton, denounced the clergy of the city. 'We know not', wrote the

---

17 Biography by G.C.B. Davis, *Henry Phillpotts, Bishop of Exeter 1778-1869* (London, 1954). Residence, DCM Audit Book.

18 Peter Virgin, *The Church in an Age of Negligence* (Cambridge, 1987), pp. 207, 291.

19 *Edinburgh Review*, No. 64 (1820); Henry Phillpotts, *Remarks on an article in the Edinburgh Review, No. 64* (Durham, 1820).

20 *Durham Chronicle*, 13 Jan. 1821.

editor John Ambrose Williams, 'whether any actual orders were issued to prevent the customary sign of mourning, but the omission plainly indicates the kind of spirit which predominates among our Clergy. ... It is such conduct which renders the very name of our established Clergy odious until it stinks in the nostrils, that makes our churches look like deserted sepulchres, rather than temples of the living God, ... that causes our beneficed dignitaries to be regarded as usurpers of their possessions, that deprives them of all pastoral influence and respect. ... Sensible of the decline of their spiritual and moral influence, they cling to temporal power, and lose in their officiousness in political matters, even the semblance of the character of ministers of religion. It is impossible that such a system can last ... and the beetles who crawl about its holes and crevices, act as if they were striving to provoke and accelerate the blow which, sooner or later, will inevitably crush the whole fabric and level it with the dust'.[21]

This was evidently too much. Proceedings were started against Williams for a libel on the clergy. The action was taken in the name of the Bishop, but it seems unlikely that Shute Barrington took the initiative: he was now an old man, in poor health, and was not much in the diocese in his last years. One would suspect Phillpotts, but the writer of his entry in the *Dictionary of National Biography* says categorically that it was not he. Williams suggested that it was the Chapter collectively, 'the Justice of the College'.[22] Whoever was responsible, Williams was charged with an attack on the Church of England, and the trial was held at Durham summer assizes in August 1822. Henry Brougham, a prominent Whig lawyer and future Lord Chancellor, delivered a powerful speech for the defence, maintaining that the Church was not immune from discussion, especially in Durham, where 'in the nineteenth century you live under a Palatine Prince, the lord of Durham, where the endowment of the hierarchy, I may not call it enormous, but I trust I shall be permitted without offence to term splendid'. It was 'the most pitiful folly for the Clergy to think of retaining their power, privileges and enormous wealth, without allowing free vent for complaints against the establishment and delinquency in its members.'[23]

Williams was found guilty, but the real losers were those who brought the case. As he commented: 'If the proceedings against us tend to awaken public enquiry into the state of the Church establishment, and if it lead to any effectual or even partial remedy for its

21 *Durham Chronicle*, 18 Aug. 1821; *The Trial of John Ambrose Williams, for a Libel on the Clergy* (Durham, 1823).

22 *Durham Chronicle*, 24 Nov. 1821.

23 *Trial of John Ambrose Williams; The Speech of Mr Brougham delivered in the trial ...* (Durham, 1822).

manifold and enormous abuses and corruptions, we shall be amply rewarded. ... Heavens! Have the Church of England come to this? We said they had no "prop in the attachment and the veneration of the people", and as if they were eager to give a proof of the truth of that remark, they apply to a court of law to supply one!'[24]

The Durham case got a lot of publicity. Brougham published his speech as a pamphlet, and wrote an article on Clerical Abuse in the *Edinburgh Review*.[25] More articles and pamphlets followed, including one by Phillpotts attacking the Edinburgh reviewer, 'who scarcely any longer pretends to regard truth and justice as qualifications for his ability ... the miserable mercenary who eats the bread of prostitution and panders to the low appetites of those who cannot, or who dare not, cater for their own malignancy'.[26]

Dissatisfaction with the Church establishment reached a new peak with the struggle for parliamentary reform, when sixteen out of twenty-seven English and Welsh bishops helped to defeat the second Reform Bill in the House of Lords in October 1831. When the third bill came before the House of Lords the following April, Bishop Van Mildert opposed it as the embodiment of a restless disposition which 'fostered atheism, infidelity, dissent and discord, attacked institutions merely because they were ancient, and sought to set subjects above their rulers'. The effect of a change such as was proposed for the House of Commons would be most prejudicial to the moral and religious interest of the people. Much of the knowledge now being diffused was superficial and injurious; it was unfortunate that 'that species of knowledge, when possessed by a person of inferior status, too often gave him an evil influence over his associates'. Phillpotts, now at Exeter, virtually accused Grey of promoting revolution and of trying to buy Irish Catholic opinion – 'a mere huckstering of pure religion for the brief, the hollow, the worthless support of men whom no concession can win'.[27]

When the Lords, under threat of the creation of peers, finally passed the Reform Bill in June 1832, only three bishops (none of them connected with Durham) were left in opposition. Of the Durham connection, Gray of Bristol had joined Van Mildert and Phillpotts in voting against the second reading, but all three abstained on the third reading. Jenkinson of St David's and Sumner of Chester voted for the bill. Fears for the future of the Church were now widespread, and demands for reform multiplied. There was a great rash of publications, fifty-one tracts and books in two years. The topics were

24 *Durham Chronicle*, 24 Nov. 1821.
25 *Edinburgh Review*, 37 (1822), pp. 350-79.
26 Henry Phillpotts, *A Letter to Francis Jeffrey Esqr* (Durham, 1823).
27 *Parliamentary Debates*, 3rd series, vol. 12, cols. 48-51, 271-87.

the familiar ones: large discrepancies in the revenues of sees, which impelled poorer bishops into holding livings in commendam or lobbying ministers for translation to somewhere better off; pluralism – sometimes the result of a benefice being too poor to support the incumbent on its own, but more often rewarding the better off and better connected; non-residence, usually the result of pluralism; and the wealth and questionable utility of cathedral establishments.

Hardly anyone advocated fundamental change in the structure of church property – calls for disestablishment were few – or the system of patronage: only some aspects of its practice were criticised. Buying and selling of advowsons was taken for granted as a very old form of property, as was the lay ownership or leasing of tithes. The object of most writers was, as one said, to make all the clergy as efficient as possible in doing good to the souls and bodies of men.[28] Conservatives, of course, argued for minimum change, seeing virtues in some forms of pluralism, extolling the contributions of underpaid curates, and the social function performed by well-born clergy bringing classes together, and asserting, in general, that it was 'better to endure an acknowledged evil of definite amount, than to incur the hazard of ills of which no one can calculate the limits'.[29] Among reformers, there was a division between those who wanted a central body to collect and redistribute surplus revenues, and others who wanted more local and voluntary procedures.

As regards bishops, there was general agreement that commendams must be ended and translations reduced; but how revenues were to be made more equal was not agreed. Equally, whilst everyone wanted poor livings improved, where the money was to come from was not agreed. And whilst augmenting poor livings would weaken the poverty case for pluralism and non-residence, there were warnings about possible undesirable consequences of enforcing residence: it might extinguish what one writer called the 'race of curates.' That some of these curates might get benefices as a result was apparently not considered.[30] As for cathedrals, hardly anyone wished to leave them untouched. They were too rich; the canons were under-employed, living in luxury (Durham's cook was singled out by one writer); the services were unattractive, cold and formal, and badly attended. 'It is impossible', wrote one critic, 'to contemplate the general state of our cathedrals without pain. ... The members of those foundations have sunk into a state of torpor and indifference, which has estranged from them entirely the esteem of the people'.

28 Edward Burton, *Thoughts upon the Demand for Church Reform* (London, 1831); James Miller, *Letter to the Right Hon. The Earl Grey* (London, 1831).

29 Rev. G.R. Gleig, *A Letter to the Lord Bishop of London on the Subject of Church Reform* (London, 1831).

30 Edward Burton, *Sequel to Remarks upon Church Reform* (London, 1832).

Cathedrals, it was said, no longer impressed men with the dignity and importance of religion. Another writer compared deans and chapters to a Upas tree poisoning all the life for miles around: 'the Christian religion can scarcely be said to exist in the proximity of their dark and deadly shade'. Cathedrals were a disgrace to the very name of Christianity, 'fortresses of sloth and ignorance'.[31] Defenders of the status quo argued that sinecures and near-sinecures were needed to tempt men of high birth and ambition to take orders. If there were no temporal rewards, low levels of persons would be introduced into the Church and the whole system would be degraded: 'no one enters the profession but the sons of farmers and little tradesmen, who would be footmen if they were not vicars'. Others maintained that sinecures were needed as a reward and support for learned men.[32] But to these arguments came the replies: If the object of a candidate for holy orders was to vegetate in a sinecure he would be a dead weight and the Church would be better off without him. Better to do without the younger sons of the nobility than continue to purchase the honour at so great a price. And as for learning, the present generation of cathedral dignitaries was not renowned for theological or literary attainments. 'The learned leisure is indeed afforded, but the immortal works are sought for in vain'.[33]

Whilst writers of an evangelical persuasion denounced cathedral services, there were some quite eloquent defenders. Was cultivated music not devotional? 'Leave us the chants, responses, anthems, to which the present spirit of piety could not object unless it objects to the practice of which the inspired author of the psalms, and the ancient Church, afford the finest examples'. What right, asked Sydney Smith, had anyone to suppose that there is not as much 'real piety in Cathedrals as in the most roadless, melancholy ... sequestered hamlet'? The only difference was that 'the service is beautifully chanted instead of being badly read, that instead of the atrocious bawling of parish Churches, the Anthems are sung with great taste and feeling'. Samuel Butler could not 'conceive how it is possible to attend the solemnities of cathedral worship, without having the affections purified, and a warmer glow of devotion excited

---

31 *Thoughts on the Church Establishment, by a Layman* (London, 1834); R.M. Beverley, *A Second Letter to the Archbishop of York* (Beverley, 1832); *Safe and Easy Steps towards an Efficient Church Reform* (London, 1832).

32 Sydney Smith, *Second Letter to Archdeacon Singleton* (London, 1839); Lord Henley, *A Plan of Church Reform* (London, 1832); Samuel Butler, *Thoughts on Church Dignities* (London, 1833).

33 Henley, *Plan of Church Reform*; A Layman, *Thoughts on the Church Establishment* (London, 1834); Edward Hall, *The Institution and Abuse of Church Property* (London, 1831).

in the mind'.[34] Butler, and George Augustus Selwyn, challenged the unhistorical belief that cathedrals had been founded for the religious instruction of the people, and the evangelical belief that the object of worship was the edification of the individual. The charge that the daily services were useless because no one attended, and no one attended because no one felt any benefit, missed the point. The question to be asked about worship was not, 'Does it edify me?' but, 'Does it glorify God?' One object of establishing the cathedral services had been to have 'one church at least in every diocese, where the daily service of praise and thanksgiving should be duly offered in the most solemn form'. Liturgy was independent of the variable feelings and dispositions of men, and it did offer opportunities for private prayer.[35]

However, even supposing that it was decided to keep up the daily services, were quite such large establishments needed? One of the most influential reformers, Lord Henley, thought the services could be performed by a resident dean with a couple of chaplains, and be made more 'spiritual'. Canons could hold livings in the cathedral city; otherwise the stalls should be abolished and the money used to augment poor livings and endow new churches in populous districts.[36] Others suggested that the cathedrals should become parish churches, with only one minister, or two or three clergy at £700 a year would be enough.[37]

Those who did not favour reducing the number of canons argued that it was good for all concerned that canons should hold benefices, not just in the cathedral city but elsewhere, alternating between the two duties.[38] It was suggested that large populous livings should be annexed to stalls – presumably on the assumption that this would make large urban parishes worthy objects of ambition, and the revenues would pay for enough curates. Or stalls could be linked to

---

34 W.L. Bowles, *A Last and Summary Answer to ... Lord Henley* (London, 1833); Sydney Smith, *Third Letter to Archdeacon Singleton* (London, 1839); Butler, *Thoughts on Church Reform.*

35 Butler, *Thoughts on Church Reform*; George Augustus Selwyn, *Are Cathedral Institutions Useless?* (London, 1838).

36 Henley, *Plan of Church Reform.*

37 *Safe and Easy Steps towards an Efficient Church Reform* (London, 1832); *Church Reform: the Question between the Church and the Country, by an Incumbent of the Diocese of Durham* (London, 1833); *Hints for Church Reform, addressed to the People of England, by a Country Gentleman* (London, 1832).

38 Burton, *Sequel to Remarks upon Church Reform*; A Churchman, *Remarks on Lord Henley and Dr Burton on Church Reform* (London, 1833); Bowles, *Last and Summary Answer to Lord Henley* (London, 1833).

poorer sees.[39] This was in effect what had been happening at Durham, the cathedral just since the 1790s subsidising the sees of Lichfield, St David's, Chester, Bristol and Exeter: the proposal was to make the practice formal.

There were also suggestions for new activities. Edward Pusey, Regius Professor of Hebrew at Oxford, canon of Christ Church, and about to become one of the most prominent figures in the Oxford Movement, proposed that cathedrals should provide theological education via a seminary in each diocese. The bulk of the clergy, he said, were at present theologically very badly educated. They took at university only an arts degree, consisting almost entirely of the classics, which was an excellent foundation in teaching men to think; but after that ordinands were only required to take about a fortnight's theological instruction; they were not required to know Hebrew or church history. And there was a serious lack of good theological writing. Cathedrals had been the nurseries of the great English divines, and could be so again. The parish clergy were either too busy, or if in an undemanding small country living, not well placed for originating new work.[40] A couple of other writers suggested that canons could take a more active part in advising and assisting the bishops, helping with ordinations, visiting parishes, preaching round the diocese, and so on. They could organise diocesan branches of church societies, give divinity lectures, instruct ordinands, make their schools more generally useful. Cathedrals should be a means of developing the spiritual energies of the nation.[41]

There was thus a large amount of advice available to the commission, consisting largely of bishops, set up by Grey's government in the summer of 1832 to enquire into ecclesiastical revenues and duties. Before I come to the commission's recommendations, I'd like to consider what the Dean and Chapter of Durham did in these years in the way of reform.

Steps were taken to augment poor livings. There were altogether 175 benefices in the diocese, of which some such as Stanhope, Bishopwearmouth and Sedgefield were rich, but nearly half were worth under £200 a year. The Dean and Chapter were patrons of 39 benefices, almost a quarter of the total. Only three of them – Shincliffe, Croxdale and Muggleswick – were worth under £200.

---

39 Uvedale Price, *Reform without Reconstruction* (London, 1833); *A Letter to His Grace the Archbishop of Canterbury on Church Reform* (London, 1833); Miller, *Letter to the Right Hon. the Earl Grey.*

40 E.B. Pusey, *Remarks on the Prospective and Past benefits of Cathedral Institutions* (London, 1833).

41 Selwyn, *Are Cathedral Institutions Useless?*; Miller, *Letter to the Right Hon. the Earl Grey.*

Grants were given to augment vicarages and provide new churches – nearly £7,000 between 1811 and 1820, £11,000 in the 20s. In 1829 the Dean and Chapter agreed to deduct a small percentage from their dividend to go to augmenting livings, and in 1832 a plan was adopted by which all livings in Chapter patronage were to be brought up to a minimum of £200 a year and the more populous ones to £350. In addition to the very poor three, sixteen livings were involved in this scheme, and consideration was also given to four where the Dean and Chapter owned a lot of land but not the livings. The scheme would cost £2,060 a year, but, it was said, would not seriously affect Chapter revenues: these were currently about £30,000 a year.[42] Grants were also made for building new churches and some parsonage houses, and money was given for schools. Altogether about £24,000 was given in the 1830s.

As for pluralism and non-residence, the minor canons were told in 1828 that a recent salary rise was intended to induce them to spend in their parishes the time that was not required by their duties in the cathedral (which only amounted to one quarter time). The exhortation had to be repeated a year later. In 1831 the Chapter agreed that in future anyone presented to a living in their gift must reside, and that no one might hold two such livings. Something was done to make the cathedral more accessible and more visitor friendly. From 1828 there was an extra service in the Galilee on Sundays in summer after evensong, with a sermon, and pews were put in. From 1833 'strangers' attending the services were handed a copy of the anthem book. At the end of 1837 it was decided to open the nave to visitors every morning from after matins to midday, with a 'watcher' appointed to preserve order. The opening hours were extended in 1841 to afternoon as well, and the Chapel of the Nine Altars was opened too. A verger was to be on duty to keep order and was to be paid extra; but when the vergers asked for more to compensate them for loss of income – presumably from tips they had previously got for letting visitors in – the request was refused.[43]

What this amounts to is a quite substantial programme of augmentation and church building, the start of enforcement of residence, and some steps to welcome worshippers and visitors. But the Dean and Chapter did not do this before they were pushed by public pressure for reform. They had had ample resources to do it sooner if they had thought of it, and they had ample resources to do

---

42 DCM, Chapter Acts; *Report of the Commissioners*, 1835; DCM, Record of Benefactions, 1858; Maynard, 'Archdeaconry of Durham', pp. 178-201.

43 Source for this paragraph DCM, Chapter Acts.

more now. The amount given annually for augmentation in the 1820s was about 20% of their income from tithes alone.[44]

The largest and most spectacular step taken was, of course, the founding of the university. This has been explored in detail by Alan Heesom in his Cathedral lecture in 1982, and by Elizabeth Varley in her work on Van Mildert. I will simply pick out the features most relevant to this paper. The story begins in the summer of 1831, when the second Reform Bill was before Parliament after an election in which the Tories had been virtually annihilated. Two of the canons, David Durell and Charles Thorp, and Bishop Van Mildert, became convinced that as soon as the bill was disposed of an attack would be made on cathedrals and Durham would be the first target. Its wealth, and the notoriety it had acquired in the political controversies ten years earlier, might seem to single it out. Nor could much help against the radicals be expected from a government led by Grey and including Brougham and Lambton, opponents in those controversies. Seeking a way to ward off the blow, they developed a plan 'to make the public partakers of our income, by annexing an establishment of enlarged education to our college'. The sacrifice entailed would be a premium to insure the remainder, and the Bishop would take a share.[45]

The prime motive is obvious, but the idea of a university did not come out of the blue. Demand for one in the north had been growing for several years, especially with the moves for founding one in London, and a quite powerful lobby was forming in Newcastle. Securing a university in Durham, funded and controlled by the Church of England, would pre-empt proposals being canvassed for Newcastle, York, and even Liverpool. The plan was worked out in the next few weeks. Some of the canons favoured only a theological college, a lower-grade (and cheaper) institution; Thomas Gaisford, who was going back to Oxford as Dean of Christ Church, was doubtful whether Durham could sustain a university with the range of Oxford and Cambridge; but Thorp, Dean Jenkinson, and Van Mildert were certain that nothing less than a university would satisfy the claims of the north, or give the public an interest in the preservation of the cathedral as something more than a splendid relic of a former age.[46] Most of the discussion had to be conducted by letter, since of those principally involved only Thorp was in Durham.

---

44 DCM, Receiver's Books.

45 DUL, Thorp Correspondence, Durell to Van Mildert, 20 Jul. 1831; Van Mildert to Thorp, 26, 27, 29 Jul.

46 DUL, Thorp Correspondence, Gaisford to Thorp, 4 Aug. 1831; Thorp to Gaisford, 11 Aug.; Jenkinson to Thorp, 16 Aug.; Thorp to Gaisford, 16 Aug.; Van Mildert to Thorp, 17 Aug.; Gaisford to Thorp, 24 Aug.; Van Mildert to Thorp, 14 Jan. 1832.

Van Mildert was at Auckland Castle, Gaisford was in Wiltshire, and the Dean was spending the summer, as he always did, in his diocese of St David's, where letters took four days to reach him

Thorp's original idea was to devote the resources of two or three stalls to the university as they fell vacant, the Bishop contributing an equal amount of money; but Gaisford pointed out that deferring the main endowment until the death or resignation of present canons put it off too long. 'Nor do I think it over generous to saddle our successors with burdens which we are ourselves unwilling to bear'.[47] Then a tax of 20% of the revenues of future deans and holders of stalls was proposed, with an annual grant until these funds became available. Then it was decided to raise the capital for the start-up by selling the freehold of cathedral property in South Shields, enough to produce an income of £3,000 a year, and this was agreed by the Chapter in November 1831. The Bishop promised a further £2,000 a year. The necessary act of Parliament was passed in July 1832, supported by local MPs and notables such as Lord Londonderry, and the first students arrived in October 1832.

Founding the university did not, however, as Van Mildert and the Chapter hoped, get the Church Commissioners off the cathedral's back. It was still intended to appropriate three stalls to the wardenship and the chairs of Divinity and Greek as present holders died. The idea seemed simple, and met Van Mildert's wish to maintain the integrity of the Chapter and keep Church control of the university; but it raised a series of problems which could not be quickly resolved. The bill to arrange for the stalls had to be withdrawn, and the funding question was left for the Ecclesiastical Commissioners, who were now beginning to consider cathedrals.[48] The first reports of the commissioners, which produced for the first time for nearly 300 years complete figures of revenues and stipends, proposed to equalise episcopal revenues by taking money from the richer sees into a central fund to be given to poorer ones, and to abolish commendams. No bishop was to be left with less than £4,000 a year; the majority were to have not more than £5,200; Durham was to be left £8,000, coming next after Canterbury, York and London. These recommendations were enacted in 1836. The commissioners then turned their attention to cathedrals. Van Mildert had continued to argue the case for annexing bishoprics to stalls as a means of providing for poorer sees. Even those, he wrote to the Prime Minister,

---

47 DUL, Thorp Correspondence, Van Mildert to Thorp, 29 Jul. 1831; Jenkinson to Thorp, 6 Aug.; Van Mildert to Thorp, 16 Aug.; Gaisford to Thorp, 24 Aug.

48 DUL, Thorp Correspondence, vol. 2; Ecclesiastical Commissioners for England, *Papers Relating to the University of Durham*, 1839; E.A. Varley *The Last of the Prince Bishops* (Cambridge, 1992), pp. 163-78.

'who look on capitular bodies with an evil eye, can hardly discover a plausible ground of dissatisfaction in thus applying a portion of them to the maintenance of the Heads of the Church'. Supposing that twelve sees needed help, two (Carlisle and Chester) could be provided for from Durham.[49] This was actually less than Durham was currently doing informally for St David's, Exeter, Bristol and Chester; but Van Mildert wished the burden to be spread, and did not like having more than a couple of bishops on the Chapter. Van Mildert also favoured annexing populous parishes to stalls: for example, the vicarage of Newcastle could be annexed to Durham. But the trend was now all towards a central fund and the end of sinecures, to the benefit of poor parishes. When the commissioners took evidence from Thorp on behalf of Durham in April 1835, some of the questions reveal that some commissioners, at any rate, thought that Durham had somehow cheated in endowing the university with money that could have been given to parishes. Thorp had to point out rather firmly that education was one of the duties laid on the Dean and Chapter in the cathedral's statutes, and they felt that the university was entirely in keeping with their objects.[50]

The Commissioners recommended the reduction of cathedral establishments to a dean and four canons. All the cathedrals objected. Some claimed that it would be impossible to keep the daily services going with this number, since a proportion of canons were aged or infirm. Two canons of Canterbury were over 80, one so decrepit that he could seldom do his duty. One Durham canon, too, was an octogenarian: he was actually quite spry. Some cathedrals proposed a scheme for taxing stalls to provide money for poor livings. Durham argued that deficiencies in the parochial system could best be supplied by annexing large populous parishes to stalls: 'Confiscation of Cathedral property uproots the ancient and solemn arrangements of the Church.'[51] Once again the issue was largely local autonomy as against a central fund. No one now argued that cathedrals should not give up anything; but, it was maintained, local resources should be spent where local needs were known. This, of course, did not answer the problems of excess revenues, and whatever the need for augmentations and new churches in the diocese of Durham (and the need was real) the revenues of Durham cathedral were excessive compared with others where the need was

---

49 British Library, Peel Papers, Additional MSS 40415, 40419, Van Mildert to Peel, 18 and 28 Feb., 2 Apr. 1835.

50 Thorp evidence to the Commission on Church Duties and Revenues, DUL, Thorp Correspondence, vol. 4.

51 *Copies of all Communications addressed to His Majesty's Commissioners ... from Cathderals and Collegiate Churches in England and Wales*, Parliamentary Papers, 1837, vol. 41.

as great. Thorp was now prepared to accept a reduction in the number of canons to six, including two archdeacons and two university professors.[52]

The Archbishop of Canterbury found the idea of taxing stalls impracticable, and several cathedrals said they would not implement it anyway, so the act that finally emerged from Parliament in 1840 resembled Thorp's ideas. It reduced the number of canons in most cathedrals to four. Durham, like Oxford and Ely, was to have six, two of them university professors. The emoluments of suspended stalls, and the separate estates of deans and remaining canons, were to go to the Ecclesiastical Commission. Deans were to reside for eight months in the year, canons for three. Benefices in the patronage of the Chapter were to go in the first instance to minor canons or clergy already in the diocese. Benefices held by minor canons must not be more than six miles distant from the cathedral city. By separate Orders in Council the revenues of the estates of the Deanery and the 11th, 1st and 2nd stalls were granted to Durham University. All existing rights were preserved: no one lost his position.

Since no one currently holding a cathedral stall was to be dispossessed, it took more than twenty years for the number in Durham to fall to six, as a result of death or movement elsewhere. Two stalls went in 1848, with the death of Gerald Wellesley and Sumner's promotion to Canterbury. Three went in the 1850s, the last one only in 1863.[53] Already before this substantial sums were handed over to the Ecclesiastical Commission from the separate estates and surplus corporate revenues, £96,000 between 1841 and 1852; but still in that year Durham's revenues were by a long way the greatest of all the cathedrals. The bishop paid over £150,000 between 1837 and 1850.[54]

The act of 1840 coincided with the death of Dean Jenkinson and the arrival of George Waddington, under whose regime much of what we see today in the interior of the cathedral was done – the removal of the Quire screen and the Father Smith organ, opening up the Quire, the Scott screen, new stained glass. In 1840 the cathedral entered its Victorian age.

---

52 DUL, Thorp Correspondence, Thorp to Grey, 3 Apr. 1836.

53 Mussett, *Deans and Canons.*

54 Maynard, 'Archdeaconry of Durham', p. 229; Commission on the State of Cathedral and Collegiate Churches in England and Wales, *First Report*, Parliamentary Papers, 1854.

Durham Cathedral is over 900 years old. Its guardians are the members of Chapter who have a responsibility to preserve the building and meet the changing needs of the Cathedral as a strong focus of Christian worship in the Diocese. Declining resources make the work of the Friends of the Cathedral increasingly important. If you love Durham Cathedral why not play a part in this work by becoming a Friend? Since their founding in 1933 the Friends have been involved in many works.

Annual grants are made towards the upkeep of the river banks, the work of the Broderers, the Chapter Library and the education work of the Cathedral.

Recent projects include the lighting scheme, the refurbishment and upgrading of the Treasures of St Cuthbert, a boiler house, and enabling facilities for those with disabilities. We are currently involved in the refurbishment of the sound system.

For further information about the work of the Friends please contact:

Friends of Durham Cathedral
The College
Durham
DH1 3EH
Telephone No. (0191)-384-5266

Enrolment may also be made at the Treasures of St Cuthbert and the Friends' Centre.

(Registered Charity No. 519110)

This book, published by the Friends of Durham Cathedral, is marketed by Durham Cathedral Friends Limited. This linked trading arm donates all its profits to the charity.